The L

– A Complete Anthology of the Dog –

1860-1940

ISBN No.
978-14455-2590-7 (Paperback)
978-14455-2710-9 (Hardback)

British Library Cataloguing-in-Publication Data
A catalogue record for this book is available from
the British Library

VDB

www.vintagedogbooks.com

Contents

Containing chapters from the following sources:

THE DACHSHUND, OR GERMAN BADGER-DOG.

This dog is generally considered in Germany to be of a pure and independent breed, for a long time confined to the mountain chain and high forests of Southern and Central Europe, extending through Germany and into France, where he is probably the original of the *basset à jambes torses*. The old English turnspit somewhat resembled him, but differed in his ears, which were more terrier-like, and also in his nose, which had even less of the hound character than that of the dachshund.

During the last ten or fifteen years this breed has been largely imported into England, where it has also been bred by the Earl of Onslow, Mr. Schweizer, and Mr. Fisher (a most successful exhibitor), and to a small extent in the Royal as well as several private kennels. Several hundred specimens have been imported and sold by Mr. Schuller, and the breed has been well tried in England as badger dogs, as well as for hare hunting. Opinions differ as to their merits in these capacities, some declaring, with Mr. Barclay Hanbury, that they are inferior to our own beagles and terriers; while others, including Mr. Schweizer—whose German proclivities may, however, render him partial—maintain that a good one will face any badger with as much pluck as our gamest terrier. The balance of evidence in my possession is, however, strongly against this last opinion, and I think it may be alleged that any of our terriers will beat him in going to ground to fox or badger. As to nose, I am induced to believe that it is, on the average, better than that of our modern beagles, who certainly do not equal in that respect the old miniature southern hounds, which in my young days used to be commonly met with throughout England.

Dr. L. J. Fitzinger, in his book on dogs, mentions twelve varieties of the dachshund, but it is generally believed that all but one of these are cross-bred. The one pure strain is that described by him as *der krummbeinige*, or crooked-legged, which is known in this country as *the* dachshund *par excellence*, and will be alluded to here only. This dog, in proportion to his height and weight, possesses great strength; but his muscular power can be better displayed in digging than in running, wherein his remarkable short and crooked fore legs render his gait ungainly and rolling to a degree amounting to the ridiculous; hence his use in Germany is mainly to mark the badger or fox to his earth, for which also his keen nose is well suited; and, as the entrance to the sleeping chamber of the former is kept as small as is consistent with his size, the dachshund is able to dig away the earth, so as to reach the exact spot, which his tongue at the same time serves to show his master, and thus enable him to dig down to it. In the extensive

1

MR. BARCLAY HANBURY'S DACHSHUNDS "FRITZ" AND "DINA."

vineyards of Germany and France, which are often on hillsides, the badger makes numerous earths, and here he is diligently pursued by the peasants, either from love of sport or to get rid of a troublesome intruder. The dachshund is also used for driving deer to the gun; but for this purpose the straight-legged cross, *geradbeinige dachshund*, is most in demand, which variety is generally also larger in size and more hound-like in character. In constitution the dog is hardy, but in temper somewhat wild and headstrong, so that he is often difficult to get under command when once on the scent. He is also snappish in kennel, and inclined to fight on the slightest provocation, or often without it. His tongue is loud and shrill, without the deep bell-note of the old-fashioned hound. The best breeds are met with in the vicinity of the Schwarzwald, Stuttgard, Lonberg, and Eberstein, near Baden Baden. Mr. Fisher's celebrated dogs are from the kennels of Prince Edward of Saxe-Weimar.

The *points* of the dachshund are as follows in numerical value and description. For much valuable information on this breed I am indebted to Dr. Fitzinger's work (kindly translated for me by Mr. Perceval de Castro, of Kensington, who is an enthusiastic lover of the dachshund), Prince Albert Solms, Mr. Barclay Hanbury, Mr. Fisher, Mr. Schuller, and Mr. Schweizer.

POINTS OF THE DACHSHUND.

	Value.		Value.		Value.
Skull	10	Legs	15	Colour	7½
Jaw	10	Feet	7½	Size, symmetry, and	
Ears, eyes, and lips	10	Stern	10	quality	10
Length of body, including neck	15	Coat	5		
	45		37½		17½

Grand Total 100.

1. The *skull* (value 10) is long and slightly arched, the occiput being wide, and its protuberance well developed; eyebrows raised, but without any marked "stop."

2. The *jaw* (value 10) is long, and tapering gradually from the eyes; but, nevertheless, it should not be "pig-jawed"—the end, though narrow, being cut off nearly square, with the teeth level and very strong.

3. The *ears, eyes,* and *lips* (value 10).—The *ears* are long enough to reach nearly to the tip of the nose when brought over the jaw without force. They are broad, rounded at the ends, and soft in "leather" and coat, hanging back in graceful folds; but, when excited, brought forward so as to lie close to the cheeks. *Eyes* rather small, piercing, and deeply set. In the black and tan variety they should be dark-brown, or almost black; but in the red or chocolate deep hazel. Dr. Fitzinger has often observed the two eyes vary in colour, and even in size. The *lips* are short, but with some little flew towards the angles; not at all approaching,

3

however, to that of the bloodhound. The skin is quite tight over the cheeks, and indeed over the whole head, showing no bloodhound wrinkle.

4. *Length of body* (value 15).—In taking this into consideration the neck is included : this part, however, is somewhat short, thick, and rather throaty. The *chest* is long, round, and roomy, but not so as to be unwieldy. It gradually narrows towards the back ribs, which are rather short. The brisket should be only 2½in. to 3in. from the ground, and the breast bone should project considerably. The loin is elegantly arched, and the flanks drawn up so as to make the waist look slim, the dog measuring higher behind than before. The quarters are strong in muscle as well as the shoulders, the latter being especially powerful.

5. *Legs* (value 15).—The *fore legs* should be very short, strong in bone, and well clothed with muscle. The elbows should not turn out or in, the latter being a great defect. The knees should be close together, never being more than 2½in. apart, causing a considerable bend from the elbows inwards, so as to make the leg crooked, and then again turning outwards to the foot, but this bend at the knees should not be carried to the extent of deformity. In order that the brisket should approach the ground as above described, the fore legs must be very short. On the hind leg there is often a dew claw, but this is not essential either way.

6. The *feet* (value 7½) should be of full size, but very strong and cat-like, with hard, horny soles to the pads. The fore feet are generally turned out, thus increasing the appearance of crookedness in the legs. This formation gives assistance to the out-throw of the earth in digging.

7. The *stern* (value 10) is somewhat short and thick at the root, tapering gradually to the point, with a slight curve upwards, and clothed with hair of moderate length on its under-surface. When excited, as in hunting, it is carried in a hound-like attitude over the back. Its shape and carriage indicate high breeding, and are valued accordingly.

8. The *coat* (value 5) is short and smooth, but coarse in texture, and by no means silky, except on the ears, where it should be very soft and shiny.

9. The *colour* (value 7½).—The best colours are red, and black-and-tan, which last should be deep and rich, and this variety should always have a black nose. The red strain may have a flesh-coloured nose, and some good judges in England maintain that this is indispensable, but in Germany it is not considered of any importance. In the black-and-tans, the tan should extend to the lips, cheek, a spot over each eye, the belly and flank, under-side of tail, and a spot on each side of breast bone ; also to the lower part of both fore and hind legs and feet. Thumb marks and pencilling of the toes are not approved of in this country ; but they are often met with in Germany. Whole chocolate dogs are often well bred, but they are not liked in England, even with tan markings, which are, however, an improvement. Whole blacks and whites are unknown out of Germany, where they are rare. In England white on toes or breast is objected to, but not in Germany.

10. *Size, symmetry. and quality* (value 10).—In *size* the dachshund should be in . an average specimen from 39in. to 42in. long, from tip to tip, and in height 10in. to

4

11in. at the shoulder; the weight should be from 11lb. to 18lb., the bitches being considerably smaller than the dogs. In *symmetry* the dachshund is above the average, as may be judged from a reference to the excellent examples belonging to Mr. Barclay Hanbury, which I have had drawn by Mr. Baker, who has caught the peculiar characteristics of the breed with marvellous truth. Though not able to show as many first prizes as Mr. Fisher's Feldmann or the Earl of Onslow's Waldmann, they are quite up to the level of those dogs, and being within easy reach of Mr. Baker, I have selected them accordingly. Their dimensions are as follows :—

FRITZ (red tan).—Imported by Mr. Schuller from the royal kennels, Stuttgard (pedigree unknown) : Height, 10½in.; length from tip to tip, 42in.; head, 8in.; ears, 7in.; age 1¼ years.

DINA (black and tan).—Imported by Mr. Schuller (pedigree unknown) : Height, 10in.; length, 40½in.; head, 7½in.; ears, 6in.; age, 2¼ years.

I append the following interesting and very valuable letter received from Germany, which, in the main, confirms the information previously obtained from the various sources above-mentioned; although in unimportant details there is, of course, some difference of opinion. I may observe, in reference to Herr Beckmann's insisting on the propriety of regarding the dachshund as used only underground in Germany, that I have nothing to do with the *intentions* of those who originally bred the dog; all that is now within my province is to describe him as he exists.

NOTES ON THE GERMAN TYPE OF THE DACHSHUND.

(By HERR LUDWIG BECKMANN, of Dusseldorf.)

SIR.—There has been a great deal of correspondence in the *Field* and other sporting papers regarding the points of the dachshund, and yet the question seems to be still unsettled. This uncertainty is rather striking, if we notice that hundreds of dachshunds have already been imported into England, and among them certainly many well-bred, if not even high bred, dogs, which might serve as a model for the real dachshund type every moment. The writer of these lines has bred and worked dachshunds all his life, and, as he has given the· subject peculiar attention, he begs to state his opinion as to what may be the cause of this uncertainty, and in what respect some English fanciers might perhaps be in error regarding points, size, colours, or employment of this ancient German breed.

1. *The Houndlike Type.*—The dachshund has had the misfortune, on his introduction into England, to be confounded by some authors with the French basset. This mistake was favoured by the fact that even our modern German and French kynologists* make no difference between the two races. M. A. Pierre Pichot, editor

---

* *Vide* Prof. Fitzinger, "Der Hund und seine Racen," p. 179 ; and De la Blanchère in his excellent book, "Les Chiens de Chasse." De la B. says verbally (p. 110) : "Les bassets sont extrêmement nombreux en Allemagne, et quelques races ont les oreilles tellement énormes, qu'elles traînent jusqu'à terre." I beg to state here that dachshunds of that kind have never existed. The French basset was identical with the German dachshund in days of yore, and was most

of the *Revue Britannique*, was the first who cautioned the English dachshund fanciers against confounding the dachshund with the basset, " the dachshund being quite a different breed."* Nevertheless, the desire for "long ears, houndlike head, and much throatiness" was going on, though one of our first and most successful breeders protested in the *Field* † against these erroneous points on several accounts. Some fanciers of the dachshund breed went even a step further, and regarded the bloodhound, with its peaked skull and "drapery-like" ears, as the *beau idéal* of our little dachshunds! (I beg to state here that the Germans have never had a native breed of dogs with head and ears like the present English bloodhound, and least of all a breed of dachshunds.)

In recent times those points are somewhat modified, but the desire for "hound-like type" seems to prevail still. In the *Field* of January 13, 1877, I find published a short scheme of points on dachshunds, from which I beg to quote the following points: "Head thoroughly houndlike, occiput very decided, ears of good length and full of fold, lips 'lippy,' nose large with open nostrils, much throatiness, and chest round without much breadth (like the bloodhound)." I suggest that the author of this scheme has not at all the intention to create a new breed, but that he really is desirous to find out the true type of the German dachshund. If so, I am very sorry to say that those points will certainly turn out to be untenable, and to be quite opposite to the opinions of most of our sportsmen and breeders. Dogs of that kind are no longer "dachshunds," but "dachsbracken" ‡ (in English perhaps dachs-talbots).

It is much to be regretted that the advocates of the hound-like type in dachshunds, who have evidently so much sympathy for these little courageous dogs, are endeavouring still to support an imaginary *beau idéal* of the breed, which neither is derived from the antecedents of the breed, nor accords in any respect with the points of our present high-bred dachshunds and their chief employment—"underground work."

The German dachshund is perhaps one of the most ancient forms of the domesticated dog. The fact is that he has for centuries represented an isolated class between the hound and the terrier, without being more nearly connected with the one than the other. His obstinate, independent character, and his incapacity to be trained or broken to anything beyond his inborn, game-like disposition, are quite unrivalled among all other races of the dog. Regarding his frame, he differs from the hound, not only by his crooked fore legs and small size, but by the most refined modification of all parts of his body according to his chief task—to work under-

probably imported from Germany into Flanders, and from there to France (compare Jacques du Fouilloux, "Vénerie," Paris, 1573, p. 89, et Verrier de la Conterie, "Ecole de Chasse," Rouen, tom. ii., p. 172). But, as the dachshund has been employed in France chiefly to hunt above ground, and is crossed with most races of the French hound (chien courant), he has lost his original frame and character, and has become completely a *hound* in course of time.—HERR L. BECKMANN.

* In the *Live Stock Journal*, 1875, vol. ii., No. 87.

† May 27, 1876, and following numbers, signed "S."

‡ Bracke or Braken is the old German hound (from Bracco); the German word *Hund* is equivalent to dog in English.

ground. It is not possible to imagine a more favourable frame for an "earth dog" than the real dachshund type, which I shall describe afterwards. I beg to say that some of our high-bred dachshunds are near perfection, according to German points; they do not want much improvement, but propagation, for they are seldom met with even in northern Germany. If I had to choose a likeness or model for these active little dogs, it would certainly not be the bloodhound, but the weasel!

The desire for "hound-like type" in dachshunds would never have originated if the natural vocation of this breed (underground work) had not been overlooked. The consequence of this erroneous idea will be that well-bred dachshunds will be regarded as a "terrier cross," and that it will be next to impossible for many dog fanciers to get a clear idea of the real type of the dachshund.

Having concentrated all varieties of the badger dog to one single class—the crook-legged, short-haired dog, with head neither hound nor terrier like, weight from 8lb. to 20lb., colour black-tan and its variations—we shall still meet here many varying forms. With some attention we shall soon distinguish the *common* breed (*Landschlag*) and the *well* or *high-bred* dachshund. The first is a stout, strong boned, muscularly built dog, with large head and strong teeth; the back not much arched, sometimes even straight; tail long and heavy; forelegs strong and regularly formed; the head and tail often appear to be too large in the dog; the hair is rather coarse, thick set, short, and wiry, lengthened at the underside of the tail, without forming a brush or feather, and covering a good deal of the belly. These dogs are good workmen, and are less affected by weather than high-bred ones; but they are very apt to exceed 18lb. and even 20lb. weight, and soon get fat if not worked frequently. From this common breed originates the well and high-bred dog, which may at any time be produced again from it by careful selection and inbreeding without any cross. The *well* and *high-bred* dog is smaller in size, finer in bone, more elegantly built, and seldom exceeds 16lb. to 17lb. weight; the thin slight tapering tail is only of medium length; the hair is very short, glossy like silk, but not soft; the under part of the body is very thin-haired, rendering these nervous and high-spirited dogs rather sensitive to wet ground and rain. These two breeds are seldom met with in their purity, the vast majority of dachshunds in Germany ranging between the two, and differing in shape very much, as they are more or less well bred or neglected. In this third large group we still meet with many good and useful dogs, but also all those aberrant forms, with pig snouts and short under jaws, apple-headed skulls, deep set or staring eyes, short necks, wheel backs, ring tails, fore legs joining at the knees, and long hind legs bent too much in the stifles and hocks.

The following points of the dachshund are fixed by the author, in strict conjunction with one of our best connoisseurs, Mr. Gustav Lang, of Stuttgart, and in agreement with some of our first breeders, with the judges on dachshunds at the dog shows in Hamburgh and Cologne in 1876, and with the editor of the periodical *Der Hund*. As these points are taken from the best existing specimens of the breed, and with regard to the employment, anatomy, and history of this dog, they may give a true picture of the real dachshund type as far as this is possible at present.

Points.

Head, elongated, large, and combined with the neck in a rather obtuse angle. When viewed from the side, the protuberance of the occiput is not much developed; skull not high vaulted; forehead descending to the eyes without any marked stop, but eyebrows raised; space between eye and ear comparatively much wider than in the hound and pointer, owing to the ears being placed high and far back; nose straight or very slightly arched between top and root, nostrils not too large; jaw neither pig-snouted nor square, but moderately pointed by a sloping line from tip of nose to the chin, and widening gradually from there towards the throat; lips short, not overlapping the lower jaw, but with a little flew at the angles. The superior maxillary bone and the jaw muscle protrude so much as to give the face a hollow-cheeked appearance. When viewed from above and in front, the skull is broad between the ears, and only slightly vaulted (neither narrow and conical nor perfectly flat; the jaw or muzzle tapering gradually from the eyes; skin rather tight over the whole head, showing no wrinkles when the dog is not excited. The shape of bone and muscles must be marked sharply and distinctly in the head, and this lean and plastical appearance (*trockner Kopf*) must remain in the head, even when the body of the dog is laden with fat.

Eyes, ears, and *teeth.*—In good heads, with long jaw, the centre of the space between tip of nose and occiput will be found to be in the hind angle of the eyes. The *eye* should be of medium size, open, bright, intelligent, and fiery (small deep-set eyes, showing the "haw," are even as objectionable in dachshunds as protruding eyes); iris rich brown in black-tan dogs, never brighter than the tan except in the bluish varieties (wall eyes). The *ear* is a very important point in dachshunds, and its situation, shape, and carriage are quite peculiar to the breed; but it should by no means be noticeable in the head from its largeness, ornamental folding, and low situation. The ear of the dachshund is set on so high that its base is nearly even with the outline of the skull and neck; and it is situated so far backwards and distant from the eyes (*vide* head), that it covers a good deal more of the neck than of the cheeks; it should be broad at the base, of equal width, and the lower edge bluntly rounded, not filbert-shaped or pointed; it should hang down quite close and smooth to the cheek, without the slightest inclination to any twisting, folding, or curl. The ears are of sufficient length if they are half as long as the head; they should not over-reach the outline of throat, and should cover about half-an-inch of the angle of the mouth when stretched gently towards the nose. There is no blemish in their being somewhat longer, but, as long as ears are neither useful nor characteristic of the breed, they should never be brought to an excess. The leather of the ears should be very thin, but the hair of the upper surface very short, smooth, and silky. In fighting and attacking, an ear of this description is drawn back and upwards suddenly, and knitted together so much that it is scarcely to be seen in front of the dog. When the dachshund pricks his ears they are not lifted above their usual level, but only bent forwards, until they stand out rectangularly from both sides of the face in their whole usual breadth, without any folding, the fore

8

edge of the ear lying close to the cheek. The *teeth* of the dachshund should be level, strong, and well shot, with sharp fangs. A peculiar arrangement of the teeth is to be found in more than one-third of our dachshunds. The two first or corner teeth of the incisors in the upper jaw are developed to a remarkable size and strength, so as to form, with the corresponding tusk or fang, a deep and narrow notch, in which the fang of the under-jaw glides. These "double fangs" (*sangengebiss*) are not to be found in any other breed of German dogs besides dachshunds. But as this criterion of the breed seems every year to disappear more, and as there are at present so many good dachshunds without this peculiarity, it cannot be regarded as a "point," except perhaps in such a case where the judge had to decide between two dogs of equal merits.

The *neck* should be long, strong, clean, and flexible. When viewed from the side, it should be finer where it joins the head, and gradually widening to the full proportions of the chest. The upper outline of neck should not be much arched, the lower outline sloping from the throat down to the protuberance of the breastbone. Throatiness is very objectionable in dachshunds, only the common dog having sometimes a tendency to "looseness" of skin in the throat. When viewed from above, the neck is wide, strong, and not too much tapering towards the broad skull.

The *trunk* (including shoulders and haunches) of the dachshund is not at all hound-like; in many respects it is more like that of the pointer, in others like that of the greyhound. When viewed from the side, it is long; the chest very deep and roomy, with breast-bone projecting; back ribs rather short, and the flanks well drawn up; shoulders rather low, with slight drop in back behind, and corresponding elegant arch of the long and deep loins; quarters not very sloping, and stern set on rather high, these dogs being somewhat higher in the hind quarters than in shoulders. When viewed from the front, the chest is very wide between the joints of the shoulder, but, being neither barrel-like nor square, it slopes gradually between the forelegs, and is rather narrow beneath at the fore-end of the brisket, but widening again towards the belly. When viewed from above, the largest diameter of the dog is to be found in the middle of the shoulders behind the joint, owing to the powerfully developed muscles of the upper arm and blade; from there the trunk narrows gradually towards the stern. The ribs spring up well behind the shoulders, and the muscular haunches project suddenly at the quarters, but not to such an extent of width as in the shoulders, even not fully in bitches. Dachshunds with narrow chest and wide hind-quarters are unfit for hunting underground: they are soon tired, and are very apt to get squeezed in narrow passages.

Forelegs very short, strong in bone; forearm well clothed with muscles; knee broad and clean; pasterns strong, broad, and not too short; feet broad, rounded, with thick large toes, hard soles, and strong, long nails. Owing to the original employment of the dachshund, his forefeet are much larger and stronger than the hind ones. When viewed from the side, the foreleg should appear pretty straight, the knees not protruding much, the slope of the pasterns not exceeding a slight deviation from the straight line, the toes not twisted or turned out too much. When viewed from above, the elbows should not be turned out (out of shoulders) nor in when the dog is standing quietly; in walking they will always be turned out more than in other dogs, When viewed from the front, the forelegs should have by no means a crippled appearance, as if the dog had rickets, or as if the legs were not able to resist the pressure of the weight of the body, and had broken down so much as to join at the knees. Forelegs of that kind will do pretty well for bassets and dachsbraken, to prevent their running too fast in hunting above ground, but not for our badger dog. His forelegs must appear as firm supports of the body, and as powerful shovels in digging away the ground, but without too much arresting the movableness of the dog in other respects; therefore the forearm should be bent inwards in a slight regular curve, the inside of the knees not projecting too much, and the inner outline of the pasterns (from knee to sole of foot) nearly straight. The pasterns should by no means slope too much sideways ("splayed feet"); if so, they will not be able to support the forearm sufficiently, and will give way every year more. All that is wanted is that the foot should be turned somewhat outwards; and this turning should begin already in the joint of the knee. Therefore, the inner edge of the knee will project very slightly in front, while its outer edge is turned more backwards. In some dogs the pastern and feet are standing perfectly straight, only the *toes* being twisted outside, which is very bad. The shape of the forelegs in dachshunds has often been mistaken, even by German breeders. They should have a simple, pleasing sweep, like that of the leg of an elegant but solid piece of rococo furniture. The bending of the forearm should harmonise with the shape of the chest, and the pasterns and feet be not more splayed and turned out than is required to restore the *equilibre*. When the dog is lying on his back the whole foreleg from elbow to tip of toes should lie quite close to his body, like the flippers of a seal. Owing to the movableness of the forequarters in dachshunds, it is next to impossible to take exact measures from the positions and width of the legs. In regularly built dogs with wide chest I always found the distance between the knees to be equal to one-third of the diameter (measured across and outside) of the shoulders. The distance between the feet (from heel to heel) should never exceed the width between the knees more than about half or three-quarters of an inch. The toes should not fully reach sideways to a line which is drawn perpendicularly from the most prominent point of the shoulder to the ground.

Hind legs comparatively higher and less powerfully developed than the fore ones; the haunches muscular; the under thigh remarkably short; the leg (or that part from hock to heel) high; the feet small, but, like the fore one, round, with thick, well-closed toes and strong nails. When viewed from the side, the hind leg appears rather straight, as it is not much bent in the stifles and hocks, that part from hock to heel standing nearly straight. When viewed from behind, quarters wide, the haunches showing great development of muscle; the legs should be wide through them, the hocks being turned in very slightly, and the feet standing out a little; but this deviation from the straight line should not be very noticeable. In

10

common dogs the feet sometimes stand out so much that the hocks touch. This is a blemish, though not so objectionable as the contrary, when the hocks are turned out and the feet in. Dew-claws are seldom met with in dachshunds, and should be removed directly where they appear in a whelp.

Stern, set on rather high, strong at the root, tapering slightly to a fine point, short-haired, length not much exceeding that of the head, and not touching the ground when hanging straight down. Carriage of stern : the root or first third should be nearly straight, the two remaining thirds bent into a rather wide curve, the slender point standing straight again, or even sweeping upwards a little. The tail should be carried gaily, like that of the foxhound, either upright over the back, or straight down when the dog is tired. Horizontal carriage is not objectionable, but it usually indicates a drowsy temper; if the stern is at the same time very thin and long, it gives an objectionable appearance, when it becomes stiff and bare, by old age of the dog. The common dog has the stern longer and heavier, the hair on its under side longer; the lower two-thirds of the stern are in some specimens nearly straight, and the last third crooked suddenly in a short semi-circle, forming a hook at the end of the stern. This is a blemish, as well as the "ring tail" and much leaning to the right or left. I have mentioned already the "otter-tailed" dachshund, a peculiar old strain—but now seldom to be found—with short, broad, or flat stern, very hairy beneath, and carried straight down.

Coat (skin and hair) : The *skin* of the dachshund is (with the exception of the head and extremities) rather full, but of sufficient elasticity to prevent looseness, which is only to be found in the common dog to a certain degree. The *hair* should be short, glossy, smooth, but wiry—not soft and silky, except on the ears, where it is extremely short and thin, the "leather" becoming often quite bare and shiny when the dog gets old. The longest and coarsest hair is to be found under the stern, lying close to the tail in well bred dogs ; and even in the common breed it should never form a perfect brush. The hair is often very scarce under the chest and belly, which is not at all favourable for a dog standing so close to the ground.

Colour : black and tan is the most ancient and legitimate colour of the class ; but this colour is not so constant as to prevent the accidental appearance of a puppy whose colour varies into any tinge or shading, produced by combination, separation, or blending of the black ground colour and the tan of the marks—such as *black, chocolate, light brown*, and *hare-pied* with blackish ears and dark stripes along the back, either whole coloured or with tan marks. Sometimes the colour of the marks (tan) appears alone, and produces the "*whole-coloured tan*," with all its varieties of shading through red, ochre, fawn, and sandy. In all the darker varieties of the black-tan dog the nose and nails should be perfectly black, and even in the brightest whole or self-coloured tan, fawn, and sandy dogs, they should be at least as dark as possible. Rosy or fleshy noses and nails indicate that there is white in the breed ; they cannot be excused by the colour of the coat —not even in whole-coloured tan and sandy dogs—or else the *nails in the tan-coloured paws of our black-tan dogs* must also be changed into fleshy or horn-coloured

11

ones. Besides, the original ground colour of the dog is black, and will appear again sooner or later in the whole-coloured tan offspring. The extension and design of the marks in black-tan dachshunds is nearly the same as in the English terrier. The tan of the cheek should not be divided in dachshunds, but ascend abruptly towards the jaw-muscle, so as to give the eye the appearance as if it was surrounded beneath by a black semi-circle. On the hind legs the tan is not limited to the inside of the legs, but extends over the whole front of them, and the half outside of the feet; from hock to heel runs a black stripe. *Pencilled toes* in the forefeet are nothing else but the imperfect repetition of this black stripe, both according pretty well to the position and bending of the extremities during the embryonal state of the dog. (The tan marks seem to be limited chiefly to those parts which are covered and pressed by the bending of the extremities in the embryo.) Pencilled toes appear and disappear in black-tan puppies of any breed in Germany; therefore they cannot be regarded as indicating a " terrier cross " in dachshunds, the English terrier being quite an unknown animal in many of those remote places in Germany where good dachshunds are bred. On the forearm and the under-thigh the black melts gradually into the tan; but on all other parts of the body the two colours should be divided distinctly, and without any blending. *White* toes, and indeed white anywhere, are great blemishes; but there are few black-tan dachshunds to be found without having at least a small greyish tuft of hair on the breast-bone, or a narrow line along the brisket, which is only to be seen when the dog is sitting on his haunches.

More rarely met with are the *bluish* alterations of the black-and-tan (for instance, slate-grey, mouse, silvery-grey, and the " tigerdachs "), which are all to be regarded as a more or less " *imperfect albinism*," originating in want of pigment in the hair. The " tigerdachs " is nothing else but a black-tan dog whose ground colour is altered only on *some* parts of the coat into a bluish tinge, while other parts have preserved the original ground colour (" *partial* imperfect albinism "), and form now irregular black or brown stripes and blotches. None of these bluish varieties can be regarded as a distinct breed, nor are they only limited to the dachshund class.* Nose and nails of the bluish varieties are dark, fleshy, even rosy or black-spotted, as the ground colour of the coat has been altered more or less. The eyes are bluish, or quite colourless (wall-eyed). All these bluish dogs should have no white marks, except the tiger-dachs, which should be as variegated as possible, and therefore white on the breast and belly of these dogs is no blemish; but they should not have white toes or white marks on the head, body, nor end of stern.

White, as a ground colour, with hound-like blotches, spotted or mottled, is much disliked by most of our breeders; and these colours should disappear entirely from the dachshund class, and be limited to the basset and the various " dachsdracken," White dachshunds are kept and bred as a curiosity, and the

---

* The bluish colours are to be found among all possible breeds of German dogs which are not crossed too much, and even in black cats. A beautiful specimen of a tiger-dachs-coloured *colley* I saw at Kyle-Rhea, near Skye, in September, 1874.

origin of most of them is very dubious. The only reason for breeding them is that white dogs are easier kept in sight when hunting a covert. But the qualification for hunting above ground is not at all the criterion of the dachshund class.

The legitimate colours of the dachshund may be divided into four groups:—

1. *With tan marks:* Black, chocolate, light brown, hare-pied; the brighter varieties often showing a blackish stripe along the back, and black ears; eyes, rich brown, never brighter than the tan marks; nose and nails black; *no white.*

2. *Whole coloured:* Black, chocolate, light brown, hare-pied; and also the tan varieties, red, tan, ochre, fawn, sandy; the brighter varieties often with a darker stripe along the back; ears and muzzle also often darker than the body; no tan marks; eyes, rich brown or light brown, never brighter than the colour of the coat; nose and nails, black, no white. In bright tan and sandy dogs the nose and nails should be at least much darker than the coat, and never fleshy.

3. *Bluish varieties:* Slate, mouse, silver-grey, either whole coloured or with tan marks; eyes, bluish or colourless (wall-eyed); nose and nails blackish, fleshy, rosy; no white.

4. *Variegated varieties* (tiger-dachs): Slate, mouse, silvery-grey, with irregular black, chocolate or, tan stripes and blotches, with or without tan marks; eyes, at least one of them, bluish or colourless; nose and nails, fleshy or spotted; white marks on throat and breast are not objectionable in the tiger-dachs.

In judging dachshunds no difference should be made between the four groups of colours, except when there were two dogs of equal merit; there the black-tan dog should be preferred, or that dog would have developed the marks most exactly in the richest tone, and with no white at all.

Size, symmetry, and quality.—The height of an average specimen is from 9in. to 10in. at the shoulder; the weight should be from 15lb. to 17lb., bitches being always smaller than dogs of the same litter. I have mentioned already that the class will most probably embrace dogs from 9lb. to 20lb. weight, owing to the different sized dogs used to hunt underground by our sportsmen. In a regularly built dog of 17lb. weight I found these proportions: head, from nose to occiput over the skull, 8in.; neck to shoulders, 4¼in.; back, 15in.; stern, 8in.; distance from ground to brisket, 2½in.; from ground to elbow, 6in.; to shoulders, 10in.; to hip, 10¾in.

In judging dachshunds it must be borne in mind that the frame of these dogs has preserved pretty well all the proportion of a large or middle-sized dog, only the legs are shortened; while in the terriers all parts of the body have been reduced equably. A cross with the terrier will be directly indicated in the offspring by alteration of the peculiar proportions of the dachshund, and therefore the badger dog cannot be called " dachs-terrier," it not being a cross. We must also notice that the reduction of the legs is not quite equal in all parts of the legs, but is chiefly limited to the bones of the forearm (radius and ulna) and those of the *lower thigh* (tibia and fibula). The consequence is that the paws of the fore-feet appear large and broad, and the hind-leg (from hock to heel) rather high and straight. These peculiar proportions become unfavourable when carried to excess; but even then they are not so bad as the contrary (too long forearms being out at the shoulders and joining at the knees, and too long under-thighs being bent too much in the stifle and hocks). The disadvantage of the short lever in the hind legs must be compensated by powerful arched loins. The dachshund runs pretty fast on level ground; he must even be able to jump and to climb, which will often save his life in steep passages underground, where an unwieldy dog is quite helpless.

A good dachshund should be built long and low, but never to such an extent as to become unwieldy. The whole outline must be most elegant, something like a weasel; head and neck carried neither quite horizontally nor straight upright.

The two dachshunds, Fritz and Dina, are pretty good representations of the breed respecting their bodies; and I was very glad to find them not corresponding much to the hound-type scheme of points proposed in the *Field* of Jan. 13. But there is something very strange in their heads, particularly in the foremost dog: there the skull is far too much vaulted, the ears are set on too low, and not at all of a dachshund-like shape and carriage. The jaw should be larger and stronger, and the tail somewhat shorter. Heads of this kind are the mistaken qualities (*missverstandne Schonheit*) in *dachshunds*, and more fit for house pets and for dogs used in hunting above ground than for an earth dog.

If I had to fix the value of the points, I should rank them thus:

	Value.		Value.		Value.
Head	15	Body	10	Stern	10
Ears, eyes, teeth	10	Fore legs	15	Coat	10
Neck	10	Hind legs	10	Size, symmetry, quality	10
	35		**35**		**30**

Grand Total 100.

Many particulars will have to remain open to conclusion till we have had a show for dachshunds only (*e.g.*, extension or division of the class, white ground colour, carriage of stern, and so on).

Where opinions differ among our fanciers, I have always added the arguments for my assertions. Perhaps my description of the dog has become too minute by these additions; but I hope it has not thereby been rendered unintelligible. I know very well that there are few dogs to be found that will agree in all respects with the particulars I have mentioned in describing the points. But nobody who is acquainted with the endless variety of animal forms will expect to find all well-bred dachshunds having exactly the same proportions. No dog is perfect, and those particulars are taken from the best head, best neck, best leg, &c., which were to be found among a number of regularly-built dogs, in order to find out the archetype of the breed, which is rarely, if ever, reached in a single specimen.

Before I conclude my writing I may mention shortly some particulars about breeding, disposition, and employment of the badger dog.

I have seldom found bitches whelping more than four or five pups; they are born with straight forelegs only the paws turn outside somewhat more than in other dogs. This would lead to the old theory of "hereditary rachitis" in dachshunds; and I have offered already a number of hopeful puppies for osteological researches in this direction, but without any noticeable success. Dachshunds are not much subject to distemper if kept in a dry, warm, and clean place. When they are full grown—say when twelve or eighteen months old—they will mostly be ready for business, when once seeing an old dog doing his work underground. By frequent exercise with rats, foxes, &c., their education will be completed sooner; but they should not be used to badgers before having reached their second year and their full development. When going to the burrows the dogs should not be allowed to tire themselves out during the walk, but should be carried in a basket in a wheelbarrow, or taken in the box of the dogcart when driving. Young dogs should always be taken up as soon as they show an indisposition to go to ground, or return too often from the earths. Many old dogs have the habit of coming out when they have received a first blow from the badger or fox. Some people say, "He comes to show his wound"; but the dog only wants to have a glance round above to see if all is right there, and, if so, he will go in again without being asked. There are many badger dogs that will kill their fox under ground, and drag the dead body out to the surface if possible; but I remember only two dachshunds who had the strength and the will to "draw" an old badger from its den, and this was only managed when they had the good fortune to seize the unlucky badger from behind in the haunches, the channel at the same time being neither too narrow nor too steep. I have already said that this is not at all the task of our dachshund, who has only to hunt and to attack his game till it quits the den or stands at bay. For bolting a fox (*spregen*) one small game dachshund will be sufficient when the shooters (for the fox is shot in Germany) have been posted cautiously and noiselessly; but, in digging out a badger or fox, one small dog will seldom be able to resist his enemy at the moment when the drain is opened, and the badger or fox is frightened by the daylight. Therefore, at least one large dog, or two small ones, should be used for this purpose. Dogs which are used often to hunt coverts are seldom persevering earth dogs; besides, they are accustomed to give tongue as soon as they come upon the track, which is the worst an earth dog can do (*weidelaut*). On the contrary, we find often good earth dogs hunting quite silent above ground till they get sight of the game.

In hunting above ground the dachshund follows more the track than the general scent (*witterung*) of the game; therefore he follows rather slowly, but surely, and with the nose pretty close to the ground. His noise in barking is very loud, far sounding, and of surprising depth for a dog of so small a frame; but, in giving tongue while hunting, he pours forth from time to time short, shrill notes, which are quickened as the scent gets hotter, and, at sight of the game the notes are often resolved into an indescribable scream, as if the dog were being punished in a most cruel manner.

15

Though not a pack hound, the dachshund will soon learn to run in couples; and two or three of these couples, when acquainted with one another, or forming a little family, will hunt pretty well together. They do not frighten their game so much as the larger hounds, and, when frequently used, they will learn to stay when arrived at the line of the shooters, not by obedience to their master, but because they are intelligent enough as to see that it is quite useless to run longer after the game.

For tracking wounded deer or a roebuck a dachshund may be used when no bloodhound (*schweisshund*) is to be had; but they must be accustomed to collar and line for this purpose, and then they are rather troublesome to lead in rough ground or coverts. They retrieve better by running free or slipped, but must carry a bell, for they are apt to keep silence when they find their game dead; and beginning to lick at the wound where the ball has gone into the body, they will slowly advance to tearing and to eating their prey.

No dog is so sensitive to rain and wet ground as the dachshund. They will often steal away from the coverts on a wet day, and sneak homewards.

Dachshunds are very headstrong and difficult to keep under command; and, as they are at the same time very sensitive to chastisement, it is next to impossible to force them to do anything against their will. Many good badger dogs have been made cowards for their whole life by one severe whipping. They must be taken as they are—with all their faults, as well as their virtues. When treated always kindly, the dachshund is very faithful to his master, and not only a useful, but a most amusing dog—a very humourist among the canine family. In spite of his small frame, he has always an air of consequence and independence about him; but, at the same time, he is very inquisitive, and always ready to interfere with things with which he has no concern. He seems to have an antipathy to large dogs, and, if they object to be domineered over, the dachshund will certainly quarrel with them. When his blood is up he will care neither for blows or for wounds, and is often bitten dreadfully in such encounters. Therefore dachshunds should not be kept in kennels with larger dogs. When kept in houses, and accustomed to children, they will make good pets, for they are clean, intelligent, and watchful, without being noisy, though often snappish with strangers.

The names which are given to dachshunds in Northern Germany are usually the same old-fashioned ones, indicating chiefly their employment or their quarrelsome disposition. For instance: Names for dogs—Bergmann (miner), Erdmann (earth-man), Judas, Krup-in (creep-in!), Kuhlmann (pit-man, miner), Waldmann (forester), Zanker (quarreller); for bitches, Bergine, Erdine, Hertha, Valda Waldine, Zang (tongs, nippers).

In England the earth dog is already represented by the various terriers, and, with respect to the great difference between English field sports and German "Jägerei," I doubt if the dachshund will ever become so useful and favourite a sporting dog in England as he has for centuries been in Germany. Foxes and their cubs are sacred personages in most English districts, badgers are comparatively rare, and the destruction of vermin is generally left to the gamekeepers. Therefore, I believe that dachshunds will be kept and bred in England chiefly for hunting coverts, or to serve as house pets and for show purposes, as an object of fashion or fancy. Both employments will inevitably alter the type and disposition of the dog as soon as his qualification for underground work is regarded to be only secondary. But I believe there are also many sportsmen and fanciers of the dachshund in England who would like to preserve these dogs as they are bred originally, and who wish to know how we in Germany are going to fix the points of this breed—as we Germans are desirous of becoming acquainted with the English points of English breeds of dogs.

To describe the real old type of dachshund, and to prevent, if possible, the creation of a new cross breed, was my intention in sending these notes.

DACHSHUND, OR GERMAN BADGER DOG.

WITH the exception of the modern Fox-terrier, it is doubtful if the institution of shows has done so much for any breed of dog as it has for the subject of this chapter. The quaint shape and peculiar appearance of the Dachshund rendered him from the first a conspicuous object on the bench, and no doubt greatly influenced many breeders to take up the breed. His admirers for the most part speak very highly of the Dachshund; but few breeds suffer oftener from the attacks of detractors, who affirm that the terms Dachshund and canine inutility are almost synonymous terms. For our own part, though we do not consider the Dachshund by any means to. be the paragon of perfection which he is stated to be in some quarters, we willingly credit him with being a good useful working dog in his own country. Conversations which we have held on several occasions with German sportsmen have convinced us that this breed is largely used in the pursuit of wounded game, and his rather slow rate of progress makes a Dachshund more especially valuable, as it enables the sportsmen on foot to keep up with him with greater facility.

The name Dachshund conveys to many people the idea that this breed was produced for the purpose of destroying badgers only, and for no other object. As a matter of fact we believe that though many Dachshunds are " hard " enough to attack anything breathing, they are not as a rule so well adapted for such sanguinary employment as for the more peaceable and less painful task of tracking wounded animals, or beating coverts like an English Terrier. As a matter of fact, we know of an English gentleman, who prides himself upon the "hardness" of his dogs, who went in largely for Dachshunds. Six months' experience of the breed convinced him that they were unsuited for the work they were expected to go through in his kennels, and he finally abandoned them in favour of Bull and Wire-haired Terriers.

As will be seen from what appears below, there are at least two very distinct types of Dachshund; and the Rev. G. F. Lovell, of Oxford, who is admittedly an English authority on the breed, actually adds a third class to the number. The Toy class which he describes is, we really think, an objectionable ramification of the other two branches, for on the Continent we have seen toys of either type, and have always considered them weeds. The two chief distinctions are the *hound* and *terrier* type, both of which are fully alluded to below; but it is worthy of remark here that in this country, singular to relate, the former type is supported by the South Country school of breeders for the most part, whilst the Terrier stamp of dog finds admirers in the North.

Mr. John Fisher, of Carrshead Farm, is at the head of the northern Dachshund world, well seconded by Mr. Enoch Hutton, of Pudsey, near Leeds, who has kindly given us a detailed description of the points of the breed as they appear good in his eyes. In the South the Rev. G. F. Lovell reigns supreme, having for his lieutenant Mr. Everett Millais, of London, though the latter gentleman has devoted more of his affection to Bassets than Dachshunds, as will be seen in the succeeding chapter.   We, therefore, consider ourselves especially fortunate in being able to give the opinions of three of these gentlemen ; for though not unanimous in their estimates of the points, the views of each party are thoroughly sustained therein.   We also propose introducing several engravings, mostly derived from foreign sources, descriptive of the breed, as, from its rapid progress in public estimation, we are of opinion that the Dachshund will soon be one of the most popular dogs in this country.

In the first place we will begin by quoting from the notes kindly supplied us by the Rev. G. F. Lovell, of St. Edmund's Hall, Oxford, who writes as follows :—

" Though the origin of the dog generally is lost in obscurity, yet the Dachshund can claim a very long pedigree ; for a dog resembling it is found on the monument of Thothmes III., who reigned over Egypt more than 2,000 years B.C., and at whose court the inscriptions state he was a favourite ; and a breed of similar appearance has been discovered by Dr. Haughton on early Assyrian sculptures.   No doubt further research would bring to light other notices of the same kind, but these show that the abnormal shape of the fore-legs is not due to disease, as has been supposed by some who have not studied these dogs.

" This peculiarity is more commonly found than is generally imagined.   Besides the Basset, both rough and smooth, and the Dachshund of France, it is apparent in an Indian breed, in the Swedish Beagle, in the Spaniel of Hungary and Transylvania, and almost certainly in the old English Bloodhound, though judges, setting Shakespeare at nought, are trying to get rid of it as a deformity.

" It has been asserted by a popular writer—' Snapshot '—that the Dachshund was not known in Germany until after the French Revolution, having been introduced by the French *émigrés* ; but however this may be, most of our dogs of this breed have come from there, and it is the head-quarters of the race.   Yet the Germans have in this, as in other cases, taken little pains to preserve the purity of the race, and mongrels abound among them.

" They may be divided into three varieties :—the Hound, the Terrier, and the Toy, though, of course, these are crossed with one another.   The first of these is more generally recognised in the south of England, the second in the north.   The third breed, which seems chiefly to come from Hanover and the adjacent countries, is distinguished by its snipy jaw, broad flat head, and small size.   It has never found acceptance with judges, who prefer a dog that looks good for work.

" Dismissing this last, then, we find two distinct types, easily distinguished.   The Terrier—which I shall pass over in few words, as I believe the hound-character to be the nearer to the original breed—is a hardy dog, with broad flat skull, short ears, often twisted, higher on the leg and shorter in body than the hound ; his stern is also not so long as the other variety. The Dachshund proper, as it would seem from old engravings, was a hound in miniature ; so he appears in Du Fouilloux for his Basset *à jambes torses* is clearly not the modern Basset, which has been developed from the ancient badger-digging dog of the sixteenth century (just as in Germany itself a large Dachshund is used as a tufter).   No one would think of putting a modern Basset to dig out a badger or fox, so that either the badger or the Basset must have altered, and evidently the latter.

" I shall refrain in the following notes from criticising the opinions of others who have written, often very well, on their pet breed, but will merely give the conclusions which I have come to after having read everything I could find, having kept and bred these dogs for some years, and having taken notes of some hundreds of specimens.

20

"The head of the hound is long and narrow; the skull conical, with the protuberance strongly marked, though I have never seen it actually peaked as in the Bloodhound; no stop; the jaw long and very strong; the teeth long, the canines curved; the eyes of medium size and somewhat deeply set; ears long, fine, set on somewhat low, and farther back than in any other breed; the nose in a red dog should be flesh-coloured, but this is to be considered only when the competition is very close; the skin over the head not too tight, the forehead being wrinkled when the dog is excited; while the flews should be moderate in quantity, but not coarse.

DACHSHUNDS, FROM "LA VENERIE."

"The neck is neither so long as to give an appearance of weakness, nor so short as to be clumsy; there should be a certain amount of throatiness.

"The chest is broad and deep; the ribs well sprung, the back ribs being very short; the shoulders should be extremely muscular and very supple, the chest being let down between them; the loin is light and well arched; the muscles of the hind-quarters should have immense development.

"The fore-legs are very thick and muscular, bending in so that the knees nearly touch, and then again turning out, so that a line dropped from the outside of the shoulder will fall just outside the feet; the hind-legs are not so thick, and many good dogs are cow-hocked. They are much longer than the fore-legs. Almost all good Dachshunds either have dew-claws, or it will be found that they have been removed.

21

" The fore-feet are exceedingly thick and large, the sole being hard and horny; the stern is long, tapering gradually to the tip, it is rough underneath, and is carried straight with a downward curve near the end, but when the dog is excited gaily over the back; the coat must be short, fine, and as thick and close as possible; the skin very thick and extremely loose. The two original colours were the same as in the Bloodhound—red and black-and-tan—but from a long continuance of careless breeding they are found of all colours; but colour in the present state of the breed should count for very little if other points be all there. In height the Dachshund ought not to exceed 10 inches at the shoulder, and a dog of that height, and 40 or

DACHSHUNDS, FROM " LA VENERIE."

42 inches long, should weigh 20 lbs., the bitches being lighter than the dogs. At the same time many of our very best specimens are a little more than this both in size and weight. The prevailing faults in this breed are too great thickness of skull, combined with ears short and badly placed; the jaw is very weak—in fact, not one dog in ten has a good level mouth, while many have a lower jaw like an Italian Greyhound, and cannot crunch an ordinary chop-bone. Others get out at elbows from want of exercise or from weakness, while some have knees bent over, a great defect; the stern is often carried too high, or even over the back. There is one more hint which may be of service to exhibitors—Dachshunds are too often shown altogether out of condition: they require plenty of exercise and not too much to eat; their social qualities and their great intelligence make them pets in the house, but the points of the breed must be brought out by hard muscle, and it is impossible for a judge to give

points for a loin loaded with fat, or hind-quarters flabby from want of work. In character these dogs are very stubborn and headstrong, not standing the whip; from this cause, probably, arises the doubts which have been suggested as to their gameness, as, if corrected, they frequently lose temper and refuse to work, but when in sympathy with their master and once excited they will hesitate at nothing.

"I add the numerical value of the points of the Dachshund :—

Skull and eyes	15
Ears	10
Nose and muzzle	10
Body—throat, neck, shoulder, chest, loins, hind-quarters	25
Stern	10
Legs and feet	15
Colour	5
Skin and coat	10
	100

"As to the use of points there is something to be said. First, they enable any one who has a dog to form some idea as to its worth; and secondly, when a judge has settled most of the dogs in the ring, either as not worthy of notice, or though not, on account of some great defect, fit for the prize, yet good enough for a commended or highly commended, he finds often he has three or four, or it may be half a dozen, dogs left in; it is then most satisfactory to compare the points of each specimen numerically, not necessarily in writing, to arrive at a right decision."

Mr. Enoch Hutton takes a widely different view of the case, as will be seen from the following description, kindly forwarded by him :—

"Very much has been written in the public papers—notably *The Live Stock Journal*—about the Dachshund, but not much to the purpose. It seemed to me that many persons who possessed a specimen (however moderate) of this interesting breed, although they had never bred a single one of the race, must needs 'rush into print,' without being able to help themselves, and give to the world *their* notion as to what an orthodox Dachshund should be; and their particular dog was held up as the correct model, which they advised all breeders to copy and aim at reproducing. Nor did it stop here: several persons who never even *owned* a specimen tried their hand at laying down the law of perfection in points, for the use and direction of breeders and judges.

"There were some few articles of relevant and reliable matter, emanating from the pens of one or two foreign writers of some experience—a few grains of wheat in bushels of chaff— but most of the articles were more calculated to mislead than to enlighten the reader.

"One of the pioneers of Dachshund lore in England was Mr. John Fisher, who has had much experience as a breeder and as a judge. Mr. Fisher's unrivalled old dog Feldmann was also the pioneer of his race on the show-bench in this country, in the days when even the judges had to be educated and enlightened as to the breed and utility of such an animal. I have myself heard a judge of some repute in the canine show-ring give it as his opinion that old Feldmann was '*nothing but a bad-bred bandy-legged Beagle!*'

"Now as to what a real Dachshund should or should not be like. He should be a *hound* in all hound-like points, the peculiarities of the breed only excepted—*i. e.*, he must have a hound's head set on a very long body on very short legs, and the fore legs must be very crooked or bandy without being much out at elbows or knuckling over at the knees, the *extreme length* from the nose-end to point of stem *should be* about *four times the height at shoulder*, and the animal should be massive, or, as some of us would say, clumsy and cloddy in appearance; in short, a big dog in small compass. The head should resemble somewhat that of a Foxhound, but must not be of so decided a type as seen in the Bloodhound.

"My plan is to reproduce the breed in its purity, and endeavour to get the best and purest blood possible to that end, but I will be no party to 'painting the lily.' It is difficult even in Germany to find really excellent specimens of the Dachshund which can be purchased, for the really pure breeds are mostly still in the hands of the nobility, and they do not care to part with even a puppy, except, perhaps, as a present occasionally to a relative or friend in their own sphere of life, or, may-be, a common specimen now and then to an inferior in position.

"The breed kept so select is preserved in its purity mostly, but in this, as in other breeds, unless the animals are properly cared for and kept up, there is no certainty of reproducing the breed *pure*. But the chances are that without such care the produce will be *mongrels*, with many of the characteristics of the breed doubtless, but still not the real thing; and I aver that many, very many, of the Dachshunds which are imported into this country are not pure-bred. But yet with some people an *imported* animal *must* be correct and pure. Even where the pedigrees can be traced back for many generations without a single stain or cross on either side, it is impossible to breed *all* correct and good.

"For some time there has been a lot of noise respecting the style of *head* a Dachshund ought to have, some breeders making it appear that a "good head" makes a good dog, and with some judges who do not thoroughly understand the breed, a so-called "good head" has been an apology for the highest awards to otherwise badly-made dogs.

"According to the new modern fancy a 'good head' seems to mean a high-peaked skull and down face, with long ears, no matter how snipe-nosed and weak-jawed the animal may be, while the rest of his body may also be faulty—*i.e.*, it may be small and weak in bone, flat-ribbed, and short of muscle; and such a one is often allowed to rule the roast at our canine exhibitions.

"Now I wish to combat this erroneous idea, and as far as possible to write it down, if it may be; and to do so, though late in the field, I will give my notions, with the rules and points by which I have been guided in my experience.

"A good head is an indispensable point with me, but there must be other grand qualities that must not be overlooked in a Dachshund; but to describe the breed properly it will be necessary to take point by point *seriatim*, and I will take the *head* first, allotting to it 25 points out of a possible 100 for perfection.

" 1. *Skull* (5 points) must be long and flat—*i.e.*, it should form a nearly straight line from the occipital bone to the nose point, and have very little stop; and I prefer a moderate width of skull behind the ears, as I find a broad-headed dog has more courage than a narrow conical skulled one: the occipital bone should be well developed.

" 2. *Muzzle* (5 points) must be long and very strong, for the size of the dog; the length from the lower corner of the eye to the nose-end in a 20 lb. dog should be 3 inches to 3¼ inches. The muzzle should be squarely cut, and broad at nose; the under-jaw strong; flews should be fairly developed, so as to cover the lower jaw, and rather more. The nose in black-and-tan

24

dogs must be black; in red dogs it is often brown or flesh-coloured, but I must own a weakness for a red dog with a black nose and eyelashes, which is attained only by crossing reds with black-and-tans.

3. *Mouth* (5 points).—The front teeth must be perfectly even, and fit as close as a vice, so that a hair could not be drawn through when closed. The fangs—one in upper and two in lower jaw on each side—must be strong, sharp, and recurved, and all must be free from canker and disease (this I make a primary consideration whenever I purchase a dog of any breed, as being in my opinion the greatest safeguard against danger from the bite of a dog). I never saw a fine-bred dog of this kind underhung; I have seen pig-jawed ones sometimes, but never kept one; and either fault would effectually disqualify an otherwise good animal.

4. *Eyes* (5 points).—These always partake of the principal colour of the coat; they must be large and lustrous, and deeply set, and in expression should be soft and intelligent; and I like them to show the haw slightly.

5. *Ears* (5 points) must be thin, soft as velvet, and long enough to reach the end of the nose, or within a half an inch of it. In red dogs the ears are generally a shade darker in colour than

the rest of the body. They should be set on low, and should hang rather squarely with the front edges close to the cheeks, and not rise at the roots except slightly when the animal is excited, or at 'attention.'

"6. *Neck* (5 points) must be long, thick, and strong, with plenty of loose skin, but entirely free from goître or enlargement of the glands of the throat.

"7. *Chest* (5 points) must be very deep and wide, the brisket strong, and its point well up to the gullet. When the dog is standing, the chest should be within three inches of the ground.

"8. *Shoulders* (5 points) must be strong and heavy, and loosely fixed to the body.

"9. *Fore-legs* (5 points) must be very short and remarkably strong in bone, and must bend inwards from elbow to ankle, so that the latter nearly touch each other, but they must not knuckle over in front.

"10. *Fore-feet* (5 points) must be very large, splayed outwards, and be furnished with large and strong black or dark-brown claws. In some specimens the claws are often worn short from walking; but if very strong this is no detriment.

"11. *Ribs* (5 points) must be well sprung or rounded up from shoulder to loin; a flatness or hollow behind the shoulders is a defect, as it shows the animal has not sufficient room for his lungs to act properly.

"12. *Loin* (5 points) must be long and muscular and slightly arched, so that it is perceptibly higher than either shoulders or quarters.

TERRIER TYPE OF DACHSHUNDS.

26

" 13. *Hind-quarters, hind legs and feet* (5 points). Thighs must be short and muscular, the legs fine and upright below the hock ; *i. e.*, must not be sickle-hocked ; hind feet smaller than fore ones ; and the hind-quarters must not be higher than the shoulder.

" 14. *Stern* (5 points) should be 9 to 12 inches in length, according to size of dog ; must be thick at base, and also thicker again a couple of inches from the base, and gradually taper to a point ; carried with a curve upward, but not slewed. The under-side of stern should be flat, and the hair should be parted and feather each side thereof sightly. A dog with a broad flat stern as described is a great rarity, and is held in very high estimation in Germany, where it is termed an ' Otter-tail.'

" 15. *Bone* (5 points) must be large, and angular at points, according to the size of the animal.

" 16. *Muscle* (5 points) must be large, hard, and particularly well developed and defined throughout.

" 17. *Skin* (10 points) must be thick, yet soft to the touch, and remarkably elastic. No other breed of dog possesses the same elasticity of skin ; the animal can nearly turn round in it when seized, or at will he can contract it by muscular action so tightly to the body that it is difficult to get even a pinch of it.

" 18. *Coat* (5 points) must be short, hard, and bright, but it varies much in hardness according to whether the animal is kept in a kennel or in a warm drawing-room.

" 19. *Colour* (5 points). The colours may be—(1) self-colours, *i. e.*, any shade of fallow, red, or fawn—the former preferred. (2) Bi-colours, *i. e.*, black-and-tan, liver-and-tan, or brown-and-tawny, as commonly seen in the Bloodhound. (3) Parti-colours :—tortoiseshell, or blue-and-tan grizzle with black spots (this colour is often accompanied by an odd, broken, or wall-eye). Hound-pied are very rare ; but though they are not difficult to obtain, they are certainly not desirable. The best colours are fallow-red, black-and-tan, and brown or liver-and-tan, which is often the result of crossing the red and black-and-tans. I prefer brightish colour in black-and-tan for show purposes, and of these I like those with red ' stockings,' in preference to those with heavily-pencilled toes, which I consider partake more of the character of the Manchester Terrier than of the hound proper. Black-and-white I have seen, and have had one very good black one ; but I am not very deeply impressed with the beauty of either.

" Having given my scale of points in detail, it will be seen that I have allotted them collectively thus :—

Head	25
Neck and chest	10
Fore legs and feet	15
Ribs and loin	10
Hind-quarters and stern	10
Bone and muscle	10
Skin, coat, and colour	20
	100

" I prefer the *self* and *bi-colours* free from white in chest, throat, and toes, but in the best of all strains these blemishes will often appear ; and for a small spot on the chest I would deduct only one point ; but for white toes I would deduct two points for each foot so marked ; and a dog with white feet or legs, or with a spot or blaze on the head or face I would

27

disqualify for the show bench, except in the parti-coloured class, although for working purposes it is no detriment whatever.

"For exhibition purposes I am a great stickler for colour and marking, as I consider it should be one object of breeders to make all animals as presentable as possible to the uninitiated public.

"I have awarded no points for size, as in Dachshunds we find that they vary considerably, some small specimens being frequently met with.

"These small ones may be equally pure, as regards breeding, with the large ones, and are often found models of perfection, and are certainly most fitted for ladies' pets, for which purpose the breed is unequalled for cleanliness and affection : 20 lbs. I look upon as the standard weight for a dog and 17 lbs. for a bitch; a couple of pounds either way may be allowed, but no Dachshund should reach anything like 25 lbs. If so, I should look for some impurity of blood, except in very old dogs, which often attain very great weights ; and I do not object to a bitch weighing 20 lbs., but I certainly incline to the smaller weights.

"The bitches are generally much lighter in bone throughout than dogs, but at the same time they possess more *quality* or beauty than dogs, as is general with the female portion of animal as well as human nature. The large dogs are best for outdoor work ; and I fancy that out of a pack of Dachshunds I could pick the best workmen by their conformation only. As to their ability, being hounds they are naturally most fitted for hunting, and possess extraordinary scenting powers, and may be trained to hunt anything, from a deer to a mouse.

"They do not possess great speed, yet they can get over the ground a good deal faster than a man cares to run ; and being slow, they are not so apt to overrun the scent, while they do not so easily tire, but will follow their chase for many hours without a break.

"In Germany they are used to hunt the deer, roe, foxes, and badger; but in the south of that empire, particularly in the Black Forest, though they use the Dachshund to track the quarry, yet when it is too strong for them to kill, the sportsmen either use the rifle or a much stronger and larger breed of dog—generally a Boarhound, or cross-bred dog— for the finish.

"In the country they are used on a small scale for hunting both alone and with Beagles. One gentleman I know often hunts fur with about six couple, and many times have I seen the staunch and true little hounds, when they come across a dry stone fence— which abound in West Yorkshire—and which had been taken by a hare, work round, seek the nearest gap, and pick up the scent on the other side, a ten or twelve miles run seeming good fun to them.

"In covert shooting they are equal to any Spaniel, and when it is very close and thick, are superior, owing to their large fore feet and powerfully built fore-quarters, though in briars their ears, head, and shoulders get severely scratched at times, and yet they seem to enjoy it thoroughly, and never flinch on that account.

"They can be broken to quarter their ground and work the game to the gun, if it be possible, and may also be taught to retrieve.

"In temper they are somewhat stubborn, and require great patience in breaking, but when once trained their great intelligence leaves nothing to be desired by the sportsman who admires the breed.

"In hunting they give mouth, but may not be so musical as the Foxhound and its congeners ; but this I prefer in covert shooting, as I then know the whereabouts of the dogs.

GROUP OF DACHSHUNDS.

29

The large paws and strong crooked fore legs are admirably adapted for working underground, while the length of head and neck combined enable the dog effectually to protect his feet when the quarry is reached, be he badger or fox; and put a Dachshund to either he will give a good account of himself. I write of the working Dachshund.

"There are some specimens of the breed which have never been educated, or that have been kept merely as pets, which would not look at a mouse even, but are for all sporting purposes quite useless.

"The dog I mean, properly bred and trained, is capable of affording sport *ad libitum*, whether in the open or in the covert. For courage or pluck I will back them against any breed.

"Cats they do not stand on any ceremony with, and I will give an instance. Some time ago we were fearfully overrun with cats, some of which came from great distances after the chickens, and often carried off full-grown bantam fowls; and one summer afternoon my little bitch Vixen hunted a very large Tom to bay in a stone quarry in my grounds. The hole or fissure in the rock was scarcely large enough for a cat to turn in, and was about three yards to the far end, and sloping upwards. Such a customer in such a corner was not easy to dislodge, and not caring to risk Vixen's eyes at such terrible odds, I caught her, and sent for my black-and-tan brood bitch Maud, 18 lbs. weight, and turned her in. There was not much noise, but in a few seconds the bitch backed out, bringing the cat firmly gripped by the brisket, while the cat's claws and teeth were as firmly embedded in her head and face, which I fully expected to see well ripped up by his hind claws; but both rolled down to the bottom of the quarry, the cat quite dead, and the bitch none the worse save a few gashes on her head, the whole taking far less time than it does to relate it.

"To give another instance of their power of jaw. I have had a little bitch only 15 lbs. weight turn a hedgehog out of a drain, and grip the prickly ball heedless of the spikes, and crush it with as much ease seemingly as a Terrier does a rat, and make no bones, or rather leave no bones whole, about it; and I have never seen even a pup of a few months old attempt to open the soft parts out before commencing the work of destruction. Young ones will worry at a hedgehog, pull it about, and make a great noise; but a staunch dog, though he may grumble a bit at the spikes, does not mind them; nor when the affair is over is there any bleeding at the mouth, unless some of the points penetrate between the gum and the teeth.

"For memory they are second to no other breed; for an affront they take a lot of coaxing to gain their friendship—(two years ago my bitch Puzzle was troubled with rheumatics, and I applied a stimulating liniment; and for a whole twelve months afterwards she carefully kept the width of the room between us)—while, on the other hand, they never forget any little kindness, nor do they require to be reminded who are their friends.

"As another instance of their sagacity and retentive memory, some weeks previous to the show at Birmingham in 1876, where my bitch puppy Dora was entered, and only six months old, I was anxious to get a pair of her milk-teeth removed, and being very fast I did not like to venture on the operation myself, but took her to the shop of a dental friend, who removed them with very little trouble.

"I had forgotten all about the affair when I called at the same shop some twelve months afterwards. The little bitch was with me, but I missed her, and at last saw her skulking against a wall about forty yards away; and not being able to understand her movements, I called my friend, who immediately remarked, 'Why, it's the little dog I drew the teeth for, and she does not care for the operation.'

" They are excellent guards, and, being on such short legs, seem, from their nearness to the ground, to have a quicker sense of hearing, and I have frequently known them give the alarm some time before longer-legged dogs took any notice whatever of the sound.

" With dogs of their own variety they are generally very peaceable, and may easily be kept in bulk in kennels, but when they once quarrel they must be separated for ever as kennel companions, else one or other will be destroyed.

" With those of other breeds they are peculiar, never quarrelsome, and hardly ever are the first to begin a fight; but if attacked by a bigger dog they will not by any means hang back, and generally come off best, as they fight low, and work among their adversary's legs and throat; while a small dog, even if as big as themselves, they will often treat with supreme contempt.

" Festus was the foundation of my kennel of this breed, and is by Feldmann, out of an imported bitch of equal character. He was shown for two seasons only, is about seven years old, and scales 20 lbs. when in good condition; in colour a beautiful fallow-red. During this time he was the winner of forty-seven prizes and two cups, including two firsts and one cup at Birmingham, in 1875 and 1876."

Mr. Everett Millais, of Palace Gate, London, who has studied the breed most carefully, is entirely of Mr. Lovell's opinion on the question of head; and in answer to a question put to him by us with reference to his views on the subject, replies as follows :—

" What is a Dachshund ?—A hound used on the Continent, more especially Germany, for the purpose of driving badgers and foxes from their underground lairs; also for the purpose of tracking and beating underwood above ground. Often and often am I asked whether I have seen so and so's hound, or if I will come and see one that another friend has imported. When I come home from the visit I think what money might have been saved if the purchaser had only gone to a Kennel Club show, paid his half-crown, and seen what constitutes a Dachshund.

" Of all people in this world John Bull abroad is the easiest to swindle. If he goes to Waterloo, bullets, &c., are imposed on him that never knew the battle-field. If to Germany, he is let in with some mongrel with crooked legs. Being an old breeder—and I may say a successful one, although I only showed one Dachshund in my life—I hope it will not be taken amiss if I say that 90 per cent. of the Dachshunds now seen in this city (of London) are no more the pure Dachshund they are represented to be than those mongrels in Paris that have the audacity to sign themselves Bull-terrier.

" There are certain breeders who, not having the courage to stick up for one legitimate type, excuse themselves by saying that there are two distinct types of Dachshunds—the Hound type and the Terrier type. This is a great and fatal mistake. That there are dogs, and alas, too many of them, with fine bone, Terrier sterns, Terrier heads, and light crooked legs, I will not deny; but, at the same time, I say that they are mongrels. They have got a root in this country, and it will always be my endeavour to eradicate it on every opportunity. The Dachshund proper is a hound, and a little beauty too. It is very easy to breed a Terrier from a hound, but it is impossible to breed a hound from a Terrier.

" The male Dachshund should weigh, when in proper condition, from 20 to 22 lbs.—certainly not more—and the female proportionately lighter. The head of the Dachshund should be conical, though not to such a marked degree as the Bloodhound. The ears are set on low, and hang like a hound's; they ought to reach some way over his nose. The Dachshund

31

possesses a good flew, and a fair amount of jowl. His neck is extremely muscular, and should stand well out from the chest. The legs, which are one of the most important parts of a Dachshund, should come down from the chest, which is broad and massive, slope well towards one another till the ankle-joints nearly touch one another, the chest dropping down to the ankles. The fore-feet should, an inch from the chest, turn away from one another, and spread well out. On no account should the joints at the ankles have a forward bend, as it is unsightly, and shows a tendency to weakness.

"The stern is not carried over the back; this is a sure sign of the Terrier type. It is carried straight, with perhaps four inches elevation.

"A good hound should measure from 8½ to 10 inches in height, and from 36 to 38 inches in length. The skin should be loose all over the body, so that on grasping the hound you find you have a handful of skin. The hair should be hard, short, and glossy.

"Colour is an essential matter to the Dachshund. I myself care little whether it be red, black-and-tan, or chocolate-and-tan, but I will have a good colour. I do not care for white about the hound, for he is far better without it; but I would not disqualify him for having it were he otherwise good.

"In red dogs, and other than red, I much prefer red noses and eyes the colour of their coats, as I think it gives them a much more pleasing look.

"One sometimes sees a mottled species like a Collie with a wall eye. It looks very funny, but in my opinion it gets this from some other stock, not the hound."

Having thus given our readers the opinions of three leading English breeders upon the subject of Dachshunds, we will, before we attempt to sum up their ideas, give a list of points drawn up by some German breeders, which have been forwarded to us. This description was published at the time of the Hanover dog show, held in that city in 1879, and was much commented on when it first appeared. It is as follows:—

The principal qualities are—

1. *General appearance*, low and very long structure, overhanging and well-developed chest, legs very short, the fore-legs turned inwards at the knees, with the feet considerably bent out. The whole appearance is weasel-like; the tail is not much crooked, and is carried either straight or a little sloping. Hair close, short, and smooth; expression intelligent, attentive, and lively. Weight not over 10 kilos.

2. *Head* long and pointed towards the nose; forehead broad and flat; nose narrow; the lips hang over a little, and form a sort of fold in the corner of the mouth.

3. *Ears* of medium length, tolerably broad and round at the ends, placed high up and at the back of the head, so that the space between eye and ear appears considerably larger than with other hunting dogs; they are smooth and close, and droop with any shaking of the head.

4. *Eyes* not too large, round and clear, rather protruding, and very sharp in expression.

5. *Neck* long, flexible, broad, and strong.

6. *Back* very long, and broad in the hind parts.

7. *Breast* broad, ribs deep and very long, and back part of body higher than the front.

8. *Tail* of medium length, strong at the root, and gradually running to a short point, almost straight, occasionally with a small curve.

9. *Fore parts* much stronger than the hind, muscular shoulders, which are short; fore-quarter very short and strong, bending outwards, the knee inwards, and the feet again outwards.

10. *Hind legs*—knuckles strong and muscular; lower extremities very short, and quite in comparison with the front legs.

11. *Fore feet* much stronger than the hind feet, broad, and the toes well closed; the nails strong, uneven, and particularly of a black colour, with a strong sole to the feet. The hind feet are smaller and rounder, the toes and nails shorter and straighter.

12. *Hair* short, close, and glossy, smooth and elastic, very short and fine on the ears;

ROUGH-COATED DACHSHUNDS.

coarser and longer on the lower part of the tail. The hair on the lower part of the body is also coarser.

13. *Colour* black, with tan on the head, neck, breast, legs, and under the tail; besides dark-brown, golden-brown, and hare-grey, with darker stripes on the back; as also ash-grey and silver-grey, with darker patches (*Tigerdachs*). The darker colours are mostly mixed with tan and with the lighter colours; the nails ought to be black, and the eyes dark. White is only to be endured in the shape of a stripe on the chest straight down.

14. *Teeth.*—Upper and lower teeth meet exactly; they must be strong in every respect.

These dogs may be considered as *faulty* which have a *compressed or conical head*, if the nose is too short or too narrow, if the lips are too long, *long* faltering ears, thin neck and narrow chest, if the front legs are not regularly bent, or if the *crookedness of the legs is so strong as not*

33

to carry the weight of the body. Further, the feet, if they are not regularly formed; if the hind legs are too long, and likewise the tail when too long and heavy and conspicuously crooked. With regard to colour, it is to be said that white as ground colour is also to be considered faulty, with the exception of what is mentioned before.

The task of attempting to decide where doctors have disagreed now falls upon our shoulders; for, as will have been seen above, the opinions we have quoted fail very much to coincide with one another. It has been our desire, however, in each and every instance, where we think a reasonable ground for difference of opinion exists, to give each side a full chance of publicity, and therefore we have devoted considerable space to the breed now under discussion. For our own part we are certainly in favour of the type supported by Messrs. Lovell and Millais, not out of any feelings of insular prejudice, but because we consider that type—the *hound* type—has been proved to be in existence for centuries. In the two earlier cuts of Dachshunds which accompany this article, and which are taken from *La Venerie*, by Jacques du Fouilloux, we notice most unmistakably that the dogs depicted are of the high conical skull which Mr. Lovell and Mr. Millais so stoutly maintain is the correct formation. Later on we come to a small cut from that *Icones Animalium* which has already been drawn upon to assist us in the present work. Here a very similar type of dog to those shown in *La Venerie* is produced, and the favourable impression towards the hound type is thereby much increased in our opinion. In estimating such matters, also, we cannot help thinking it advisable to turn one's thoughts in the direction of the uses to which a breed is put. In so doing, our views concerning the hound type have been greatly strengthened from the reflection that, as we have already said, tracking game is the Dachshund's forte, not baiting savage vermin in the latter's native earth. One remark, too, of Mr. Millais's has struck us very forcibly. " It is very easy to breed a Terrier from a hound, but it is impossible to breed a hound from a Terrier." Without going the entire length of Mr. Millais as to the impossibility of the latter achievement in breeding, we readily accept its difficulty, and recognise the force of the argument he makes use of.

We are not, however, wholly at one with Mr. Millais in his sweeping condemnation of the Terrier type. We prefer the hound type of Dachshund as being in our opinion the older and the more characteristic of the two; but in the face of what we have seen and heard, it is impossible to ignore the existence of the Terrier type, and the store set upon it in certain parts of its native country—Hanover to-wit. How this class of dog originated, except by crossing the hound type of Dachshund with a Terrier, we cannot tell; but as it now exists it is impossible to decline to recognise it as a variety, though perhaps an undesirable one, of the breed. A satisfactory illustration of this class of dog will be seen in the engraving, and our readers who are ignorant of the different types will thereby be able to form their own opinions on the beauty of the Terrier type of dog.

Another point on which Mr. Everett Millais and Mr. Enoch Hutton break a lance is that of the colour of the red Dachshund's nose. Here, as in Germany, considerable difference of opinion exists; but we personally feel no hesitation in offering our allegiance to the party which advocates red noses, as black noses in such cases look quite out of keeping with the colour.

There remains one description of Dachshund which has been quite overlooked by Messrs. Lovell, Millais, and Hutton, and which is rarely seen in this country, and that is the rough-coated variety, which will be found to be represented in the engraving on the preceding page. This breed, no doubt, is but a cross from the original variety, and is not valued in its native country by admirers of the breed.

From what has been said and written concerning the breed from time to time by various authorities, it will be seen that it is not only on the subject of type that their admirers differ. Enthusiasts, as we have before remarked, give this breed of dog credit for an amount of gameness which we scarcely think it fully deserves. It is no doubt true that instances of exceptionally game Dachshunds have come beneath the observation of gentlemen who have studied the breed, as in the cases Mr. Enoch Hutton quotes ; but we are inclined to imagine that these are exceptions rather than invariable rules. As house-dogs Dachshunds are without superiors, as their voices are deep enough to awaken the heaviest sleeper, and their sense of hearing is very acute.

In consequence of the fast-increasing number of these dogs which appear at the principal dog shows, efforts have been made to gain additional classes for them, as they are usually divided according to *colour* only. Classes for Dachshunds black-and-tan, and Dachshunds other than black-and-tan, have been up to the time of writing (1880) the order of the day, and no doubt during the earlier stages of this variety's existence as a show dog were amply sufficient. As, however, so many specimens of either type appear, certain exhibitors have been trying to gain classes for each variety of their favourite dog, with apparently some chance of ultimate success. The efforts of these breeders, however, are not regarded with favour by the supporters of the hound type of Dachshund, who maintain that the Terrier type is a mongrel unworthy of support, and therefore advocate the institution of heavy weight and light weight classes, instead of a division of the types. How things will work it is impossible to foretell ; but an indisputable fact in connection with the Dachshund is its fast-increasing popularity amongst us, and its admirers appear to spare no trouble or expense in importing the best blood into the country.

Having now come to the end of our notes on the Dachshund, we can but once more repeat that our sympathies lie with the class of dog so ably depicted by the Rev. G. F. Lovell ; but under any circumstances we would caution breeders against crossing the two types together, as certain ruin will be caused to each thereby. In breeding, we may remark that liver-coloured puppies frequently appear when reds are bred together. This colour, though disliked for show purposes, is often very valuable for crossing when increased depth of colour is required, and therefore a liver-coloured brood bitch or two is often seen in breeders' kennels. Whilst on this subject of colour we may remark that we cordially endorse the views already given on the subject of white. It is most undesirable that white blazes on the head or chest should ever be seen, and white feet we regard almost as a disqualification. In Germany we have seen many of the breed marked similarly to hounds, but cannot recall any to memory which were black-and-tans or fallow-reds marked with white. As regards the black ones, Mr. Mackenzie, of Perth, in 1879, imported a very handsome dog of this colour who rejoices in the name of Gravedigger. This dog was a good winner in his own country, and has done his master good service in the land of his adoption, and we do not know of a better-coated one, his skin being everything that could be desired.

Amongst the leading Dachshund breeders and exhibitors of the day the names of the Rev. G. F. Lovell, Mr. John Fisher, Mr. Everett Millais, Mr. W. Arkwright, and Mr. Enoch Hutton, are the most prominent, the first-named gentleman having been the owner of what is still considered to have been the best Dachshund ever seen in this country. We allude to Pixie, a wonderful little bitch, whose untimely death alone prevented her appearing in our coloured plate. Mr. John Fisher's Feldmann was truly, as Mr. Hutton says, the pioneer of his variety in this country, and Mr. Hutton's Festus, whose portrait is in our coloured plate, is recognised as a grand specimen of his type. Mr. Millais has not shown much, but has good dogs; and Mr. Arkwright's Xaverl was for a long time champion of his breed.

The dogs selected for illustration in the coloured plate are—

Major Cooper's (of Pitsford Hall, Northampton)`Waldmann, an extremely good specimen of the black-and-tan variety, who is a winner at some of our best shows.

The Rev. G. F. Lovell's Schlupferle. A handsome fallow-red, whose measurements are as follows:—Length from tip of nose to stop, 3 inches; from stop to occiput, 4¾ inches; length of back from top of shoulders to setting on of stern, 16 inches; girth of thigh, 9 inches; girth of fore-arm, 5 inches; girth of pastern, 3½ inches; height at shoulders, 12 inches; height at elbows, 6½ inches; height at loins, 13½ inches; height at hock, 4½ inches; length of stern, 11 inches; weight, 23 lbs.; age, 4 years 10 months.

Mr. Enoch Hutton's Festus, already alluded to by his owner in the notes with which he obliged us as above.

The large full-page illustration of Dachshunds at work is the production of a celebrated foreign artist, who is especially happy in conveying the expression of animals to paper.

Following our usual custom, we shall now append a scale of points for judging the breed, which we cheerfully admit are founded upon the scale afforded us by Mr. Lovell in the preceding portion of this chapter :—

STANDARD OF POINTS FOR JUDGING DACHSHUNDS.

	Value.
Skull and muzzle	10
Ears and eyes	5
Shoulders and chest	5
Loins	5
Fore legs and feet	5
Hind legs and feet	5
Colour and coat...	5
General appearance, including skin	10
Total	50

DACHSHUNDS.

38

THE DACHSHUND.

WHETHER we shall ever get another dog from the Continent that, within so few years, has spread, multiplied, and become so much one of ourselves as the dachshund, is an open question. His disposition was genial, his habits were of the best, but he was quaint in look, and, if not so autocratic in appearance as the Borzoi, he trotted behind his master or mistress, with all the airs that follow high life, conveying an impression that he alone had the right to be where he was. Then, again, he was not a fighting dog, and, though excellent as a " watch and guard," he was not ill-natured, and his skin felt so soft and velvety that it became pleasanter to pat and stroke him than to do the same with a Dandie Dinmont terrier or another pet terrier that was said to be brought from the Isle of Skye; and he certainly appeared to be two animals rolled into one—a hound and a terrier—perhaps he is the connecting link between the two breeds.

With such qualifications he soon became a favourite, and from being represented in couples in the variety class at our dog shows he speedily appeared in scores, and had, as he has now, many separate divisions provided for him—challenge cups, and other valuable prizes, and a specialist club to look after his welfare to boot. These remarks, and subsequent ones, are in connection with the smooth-coated little hound as we acknowledge him, and do not include the rough-haired variety that has occasionally been seen here, and is pretty common in some parts of the German Empire.

Who was responsible for bringing the first dachshund to England I do not know, any more than I am acquainted with the particulars of the origin of the dog itself. Some sporting men of the old school have said he was nothing more than the common turnspit, which the cooks of their grandparents had used in their kitchens to turn the spit in which their joints and geese and turkeys were roasted. Perhaps there had been some connection between the two breeds; there was a resemblance, for both had short crooked legs and unduly long bodies, but the cooks' dogs were seldom whole coloured, as is pretty nearly always the case with the dachshund, at least with our British variety.

No doubt either the dachshund himself, or a dog

very like him, perhaps it was the turnspit, was known in the East long before the Christian era. Egyptian and Assyrian sculptures, some of them 2000 B.C., depict a dog much after his stamp, but whether he was then used as a sporting dog or as a companion, or to assist in culinary operations, we are not told, all we know is that at the court of King Thothmes III. he was a favourite. Since that period he has undergone many modifications. Even within the past quarter of a century, during his association with our English dogs, his character has changed somewhat. In Germany, Belgium, and other parts of the Continent, from whence he came to us, he is used as a sporting dog, to draw or drive the fox and badger, but here he is for the most part fancied as a companion and for exhibition purposes, and his rapid growth to popularity is evidence of his excellence in both respects. Still, even our English dachshunds will do their work well when properly trained to the duty.

Comparatively few of our dachshunds have any chance of showing how good they are at sport. If properly entered they have no superiors at their legitimate game of going to ground to fox and badger, when the latter have to be dug out. I do not for a moment suggest that they will bolt a hunted fox as quickly as a huntsman's terrier—that is not their game.   All the dachshund professes to do is to find the fox or badger in his earth and remain there until you can dig to him.   He makes no attempt to fight or attack the "varmint," but simply barks at it incessantly.   Then if the game does turn his back upon his plucky little opponent, the latter immediately proceeds to business by a fierce attack in the rear, which is discontinued when the fox or badger turns again and faces the hound.

This description of work, of course, enables the hunters to dig with great accuracy in the direction the fox or badger lies, and the wary dachshund is rarely badly hurt, whereas the terrier that gets to close quarters with a badger, in his natural earth, will, as a rule, get terribly mauled.   Still, I have had fox terriers that would bark and bark until the game budged, but this barking is not always good enough to drive a fox, and under no circumstances will it send either otter or badger into the open.   Particulars of a few day's sport with dachshunds appear at the end of this chapter.

When duly entered the dachshund makes an excellent line hunter, and Mr. Harry Jones, of Ipswich, tells me that his bitch Juliet was regularly hunted with a pack of Basset-hounds, and was about the most reliable of the lot.   Of course, one has not to go further for an instance of the general gameness of the dachshund race than the trials with them on the Continent at both foxes and badger, which the best dogs have to treat much in the same manner as our terriers have to do here on certain occasions. It is quite the custom for such trials to be arranged at certain dog shows in Belgium and Germany for the delectation of English visitors, who, however, do not as a rule take particularly kindly to what some persons consider quite a high branch of sport.

About the period when the dachshund was gaining its popularity here, considerable correspondence about him took place in the *Field* as to what he was and what he was not, and, if I make no mistake, Mr. Barclay Hanbury, Mr. John Fisher (Cross Hill, Leeds), and others, gave their opinions on the subject. However, notwithstanding the complications likely to ensue on the introduction of a new breed, especially when one authority quoted Dr. Fitzinger, who said there were twelve varieties of the dachshund—a statement fortunately qualified by the remark that they were mostly cross-bred—all went well. In due course something like the correct article was fixed upon, and from that we have our dogs of the present time. As a fact I see less discrepancy in the type of the modern dachshund than is to be noticed in some other purely English breeds—the fox terrier, to wit.

Although some of our best dogs are accepted by German authorities as excellent specimens, still our British breeders have in a degree constructed a line of their own, and where, on the Continent at any rate, two varieties were acknowledged, the hound type and the terrier type, here a happy medium has been struck, and the handsome dog now seen on our show benches is the result. I have a large amount of information as to the work and general description of the quaint little dog as he is seen in Germany, and where he divides national favouritism with the Great Dane, but I fancy, in a book dealing with British dogs alone (and those that we have made such by fancy or manipulation) it will be best not to trespass on foreign ground. The Germans especially do well by their favourite dog, and the Dachshund Stud Book published by them is certainly, for completeness and tasteful elaboration, ahead of anything of the kind we have in England. As an instance of what is done in this particular, it may be mentioned that where the dog alluded to is red in colour, particulars of him are printed in red ink, and where he is black and tan the usual black ink is used. The same arrangement applies to the portraits of dogs, with which the pages of this Stud Book are thickly interspersed.

Some twenty years ago Herr Beckmann, one of the German authorities, dealing with the different types of the breed, wrote as follows :

" Having concentrated all varieties of the badger dog to one single class—the crooked-legged, short-haired dog, with head neither hound nor terrier like, weight from 18lb. to 20lb., colour black-tan and its variations—we shall still meet many varying forms. With some attention we shall soon distinguish the *common* breed and the *well* or *high-bred* dachshund. The first is a stout, strong-boned, muscularly built dog, with large head and strong teeth; the back not much arched, sometimes even straight; tail long and heavy; forelegs strong and regularly formed ; the head and tail often appear to be too large in the dog; the hair is rather coarse, thick-set, short, and wiry, lengthened at the underside of the tail, without forming a brush or feather, and covering a good deal of the belly. These dogs are good workmen, and are less affected by weather than high-bred ones; but they are very apt to exceed 18lb. and even 20lb. weight, and soon get fat if not worked frequently. From this common breed originates the well and high-bred dog, which may at any time be produced again from it by careful selection and inbreeding without any cross. The *well* and *high-bred* dog is smaller in size, finer in bone, more elegantly built, and seldom exceeds 16lb. to 17lb. weight; the thin, slight tapering tail is only of medium length; the hair is very short, glossy like silk, but not soft; the under part of the body is very thin haired, rendering these nervous and high spirited dogs rather sensitive to wet ground and rain. These two breeds are seldom met with in their purity, the vast majority of dachshunds in Germany ranging between the two, and differing in shape very much, as they are more or less well-bred or neglected. In this third large group we still meet with many good and useful dogs, but also all those aberrant forms, with pig snouts and short under jaws, apple-headed skulls, deep set or staring eyes, short necks, wheel backs, ring tails, fore-legs joining at the knees, and long hind legs bent too much in the stifles and hocks."

That we have not the latter in this country can with truth be stated, and I think the majority of the best dogs with us now will quite equal the standard of the best dogs as laid down by Germany's great authority.

So far as my judgment goes, English breeders like Mr. W. Arkwright, Mr. M. Wootten, Mr. A. W. Byron, Mr. H. Jones, Mr. A. O. Mudie, Mr. H. A.

Walker, Captain and Mrs. Barry, Miss A. G. Pigott, Mr. E. S. Woodiwiss, Mr. N. D. Smith, Miss Ramsbottom, and others, have produced dachshunds quite equal to any that have appeared of late years at the leading Continental exhibitions, although, naturally, more specimens are bred there than with us.

Mr. Jones believes our modern dachshunds are far more typical than they have ever been, and with this opinion I thoroughly coincide. There may be cases in which legs, feet, chest, and loin have been neglected in trying to produce beautiful heads, but this has not been carried out to any great extent. The best dachshunds of to-day are particularly sound, have excellent chest and loins, and, considering their short legs and long bodies, get over the ground at almost an extraordinary rate, and such animals as Mr. Jones's Pterodactyl, Jackdaw, and Jim Crow; Miss Pigott's Primula, Prima Donna, and Belle Blonde; Mrs. Nugent's Widgeon; Mr. Woodiwiss's Wiseacre, and some others which could be mentioned, are quite able to more than hold their own at any of the Continental shows.

Although, as I have previously stated, the dachshund is usually kept in this country as a companion and for show purposes, he is quite capable as a sporting dog. Personally I have never seen one of the little hounds at work, so for information as to their abilities in this respect I cannot speak of my own knowledge—so Mr. Jones kindly acceded to my wishes and furnished the following very interesting account of three or four days badger hunting with dachshunds of his own. That they acquitted themselves with credit no one will deny, and at any rate performed their duties as well as our terriers would have done under similar circumstances.

"I had some excellent sport with dachshunds in the spring of 1878. I arranged to pay three visits to friends, all of whom promised to introduce me to some badgers in their wild state. I started for Gloucestershire with two couples of dachshunds, each about three years old and well used to going to ground. The first time we went out was on the Wednesday before the Good Friday. It was full moon, and the night was very bright and still. In addition to the four dachshunds my friends ran four terriers. The earthstopper had gone on before and stopped all the main earths, and remained by them until we came. We did not net any of the places, our object being to run a badger to ground in a small earth and dig him out.

"From 2 a.m. to 5 p.m. the little pack hunted well, and were very merry sometimes ; but it was the thickest underwood I was ever in. When you left a ride you were lost amid the tangle of brambles. A badger was viewed once, and had a sharp tussle with one of the terriers. The dachshunds kept well together, and on one occasion hunted out in the open for a long way, but I think they were then on the line of a fox. However, at about 5 a.m. it was found that one of the main earths had been unstopped and two of the terriers could be heard hard at it in different places. Being well supplied with digging appliances we commenced operations, and about 10 a.m. had dug to one of the terriers, which we found terribly torn and bitten. After getting the terrier out, a dachshund was put in, and we soon saw him backing slowly out, and, to our astonishment, he brought with him a young badger, not quite half grown, dead and nearly cold. This the terrier must have killed early in the morning.

" The dachshund was sent to ground again, and he was soon heard baying close to where we had heard the other terrier, but his voice was so loud we could tell exactly where he was.

" Then, by twelve o'clock, we had dug to the second terrier, and he was more injured than the first, so they were both sent home.

" The badger now seemed to shift his quarters,

for, on putting a second dachshund in, we heard both dogs baying close together in a different place, and, after the quietness of the terriers, the loud baying of the dachshunds seemed to encourage the men in their digging, for there was no doubt as to the whereabouts of the dogs. About 3 p.m. we dug down to them, and soon bagged a very fine badger.

" Knowing, however, that there was more than one badger in, for the terriers had been working at different places, the four dachshunds were all sent underground together. They could not find the other badger, but one of them brought out another half grown one that had been killed by the terriers.

" I left that night (Thursday) for Monmouthshire and after midnight on Good Friday we started off with the four little hounds and a couple of rough haired terriers for some very large woods, but with good rides in them. All the earths were well attended to with faggot bundles, the last of them was being stopped when we arrived. The night was cloudy and occasionally quite dark, but the dogs hunted very well, and were close on to a badger several times, but failed to mark one to ground. About 6 a.m. the dachshunds (both terriers had been badly bitten in the wood, and were sent to the inn) took a line towards the river Usk. This line they hunted very prettily for a long way, when two of them went to ground by the riverside in an earth about six feet below the top of the bank, and in a moment they were baying in a way that left no doubt they were at something. I was half afraid it might be a fox, but some hairs picked off the side and top of the entrance proved it was used by badgers; and the unmistakable imprint of the badger's nails, quite fresh, close to the entrance, settled the question.

" Before commencing digging, the men expressed a great wish to send to the village for a noted terrier that was there; but this we would not permit, and they did not hesitate to say they had no confidence in a dachshund at a ' dig out,' but how they had reason to change their opinions will be told later on.

" The earth ran nearly straight under the field, not more than some five or six feet deep, and the loud voices of the dachshunds could very plainly be heard baiting their game. We cut a trench right across what we thought would be about the end of the earth, leaving plenty of room to work; but just as we broke into the earth the badger went 10 or 12 feet further underground, the dogs following him close up. Thus there was nothing for it but to dig another trench, having first securely stopped the earth towards the river. This second trench cut right into the end of the earth, and but for the spade touching the badger we should have bagged him then, but he went forward facing the dogs, and remained about half way between the two trenches.

" I then put the other two dogs in from the end of the earth, and at it they went, and whichever way the badger faced he was attacked in the rear.

" He showed himself several times at the mouth of the hole, but we missed him with the tongs. At last he made a bolt in a hurry, and over went the man with the tongs, who was then on his knees, looking down the hole, and, jumping up the corner of the trench, the badger made for the river bank.

" A shepherd had come to look on, and, having his sheepdog with him, the latter immediately gave chase, catching up to the badger just as he reached the edge of the bank. The badger landed beauti-fully on the narrow ledge upon which the earth opened, but the poor sheepdog went right over down to the bed of the river, a fall of nearly twenty feet. The dachshunds were helped out of the trench, everyone ran and halloaed, and there was great excitement. The badger turned up in a dry ditch full of brambles, and, by the combined aid of the dachshunds and the sheepdog, was ultimately bagged.

"On the Monday I was driven about fourteen miles for a third hunt, as my friend had seen a badger quite recently in the wood, and had made all arrangements for stopping the earths. I took the recently caught badger with me, as it was wanted to turn down, and the one we had bagged on the Thursday was of the wrong sex. The moon was late in rising, so we did not leave the house until 2.30 a.m. on Tuesday. The earth-stopper had all the main earths stopped, and a fire burning in front, by which he had made himself comfortable.

"This night we had only the four dachshunds; they did a lot of hunting, several times running well, and giving plenty of music. They worked round the big wood twice, and when near the middle two badgers were seen quite close together, one following the other, and not far behind was old Waldmann, throwing his tongue freely on their line. My friend gave a view holloa that could be heard all up the hillside, and soon afterwards these two badgers were run to ground in a small earth. Waldmann got in before he could be taken up, and I could not get him out. I had particularly wanted to run a red bitch that had not done much work.

"We again dug a trench right across the line of

the earth beyond where we judged the badgers to lie. To prevent them making a bolt we stopped the earth behind the dog with a large stone, leaving only a small hole to admit the air. We dug right on to the nose of one badger, which itself was digging as hard as it could, and had nearly buried himself, still we got it. Then we cleared the earth out, and in trying to get hold of the second with the tongs caused it to make a drive at poor old Waldmann, who was blocked in by the stone. The dog received an ugly bite, but we soon had our second badger in the sack.

" I returned that night with only one damaged dog, and three very successful ' dig-outs.'

" When we went to the stables for the dogs and Saturday's badger, and had not very much time for the train, we discovered our badger had got out of the box, and was not to be found. A cast round with the dogs and they marked him up the chimney in the harness room; he had reached a ledge in the flue, and get him down we could not, so had to leave him. He was ultimately taken and sent on, and I believe helped to make several good earths that are now used by foxes.

" The following moon I took the same four dachshunds into Warwickshire, where I had often been with my terriers on former occasions ; but this was the first introduction of the dachshunds. We tried to run a badger into the nets, but were not successful, though the dachshunds found one in the meadows, and had some capital hunting before they lost him. There were a lot of rabbits about here, and I rather think they caused our hounds to run riot a little.

" After breakfast we had a walk round all the likely places where the badgers might have gone, taking a hardy-looking terrier with us, one, however, too big to get to ground. About 10 a.m. the dachshunds marked a badger in a nice little earth, and, before lunch, we had him in a sack; one man was bitten in the thumb by the badger, and our host was bitten in the leg by a dachshund. In the excitement of ' bagging ' he picked one of the dachshunds up by the tail, flinging him under his arm, and was stooping down and picking up another, when No. 1 pinned him in the calf of the leg. Needless to say he dropped the two dogs.

" The biting for that day was not yet over, for, when talking at lunch of taking the badger on the bank of the Usk, the question was raised, could the four dachshunds so hamper a badger in the open as to enable him to be taken with the tongs? Nothing would satisfy the party but a trial, so the badger was turned out in a very hilly field, when he made off up hill, and from the way in which he bowled the dach-shunds over, I have no doubt he would have got away, had not the big terrier been slipped. During the process of getting hold of the badger, a terrier puppy, about nine months, came up from the house, and hearing a great deal of 'loo loo,' and not know-ing quite what to do, quietly seized the man who was energetically trying to get hold of the badger with the tongs, and left his mark on him.

"I have had many such days, of which the above are fair examples, and from these results am quite convinced that for digging out a fox or badger, nothing can beat a properly entered dachshund."

Although new breeds of dogs are being intro-duced, I fancy that the dachshund will continue to hold his own, for he is by no means difficult to rear from puppyhood, and, as I have already stated, is a desirable dog as a companion. He is, moreover, one of the canine favourites of Her Majesty the Queen at Windsor. Seldom used for his particular work in this country, nor for hunting in packs, for our beagles and harriers will do the latter better than he, and, for going to ground after fox or badger or otter we have our own terriers, which we cannot afford to lose; still the dachshund has deservedly popularised himself, and when in his puppydom he has chased a sheep or made a raid on the poultry yard, it is no more than other young untrained dogs of our own have done and will do to the end.

The fact that the dachshund has a peculiarly nice skin makes him specially adaptable as an agreeable pet dog; and when to this is added a pleasant face, an endearing disposition, and, for a hound, a tolerable immunity from the aroma of the kennel, there is little wonder he has become popular.

What a dachshund in the flesh is like, Mr. Wardle's drawings at the commencement of this chapter plainly tell, and the following standard, drawn up by the Club, will give additional knowledge to the searchers for information.

" *Head and skull.*—Long, level, and narrow; peak well developed; no stop; eyes intelligent, and somewhat small; follow body in colour.

" *Ears.*—Long, broad, and soft; set on low and well back; carried close to the head.

" *Jaw.*—Strong, level and square to the muzzle; canines recurvent.

" *Chest.*—Deep and narrow; breast bone prominent.

" *Legs and Feet.*—Fore legs very short and strong in bone, well crooked, not standing over; elbows well clothed with muscle, neither in nor out; feet large, round, and strong, with thick pads and strong nails.   Hind legs smaller in bone and higher, hind feet smaller.   The dog must stand true, *i.e.*, equally on all parts of the foot.

"*Skin and Coat.*—Skin thick, loose, supple, and in great quantity; coat dense, short and strong.

"*Loin.*—Well arched, long and muscular.

"*Stern.*—Long and strong, flat at root, tapering to the tip; hair on under side coarse; carried low except when excited.   Quarters very muscular,

"*Body.*—Length from back of head to root of stern, two and a half times the height at shoulder. Fore ribs well sprung, back ribs very short.

"*Colour.*—Any colour, nose to follow body colour; much white objectionable.

"*Symmetry and quality.*—The dachshund should be long, low and graceful, not cloddy.

Head and skull	12		Ears	6¼
Jaw	5		Chest	7
Legs and feet	20		Skin and coat	13
Loin	8		Stern	5
Body	8½		Colour	4
Symmetry and quality	11			
	64½			35½

Grand Total 100.

"The weight: Dogs about 21lb., bitches about 18lb.

"The Dachshund Club do not advocate point judging, the figures are only used to show the comparative value of the features."

It will be noticed in the above Club description that "any colour" is allowed, with only the proviso that "much white is objectionable." The accepted colours with us are red, black and tan, chocolate (or brown), and chocolate and tan. There is some variation in the shades of hue, especially amongst the reds, some of which are so pale as to be almost yellow. The black and tans and the deeper reds are the handsomest, and a white foot or feet and a little white on the breast are no detriment. "Mouse" coloured specimens are occasionally met, sometimes with tan shadings, sometimes without. This is not a desirable colour, and "wall" or "china eyes" often accompany it. Then we have the marbled or mirled varieties, tortoiseshell they are often called, but most frequently "dappled," and under the latter name classes are repeatedly provided for them at our leading shows. They are, however, not particularly well filled, though Mr. E. S. Woodiwiss usually sends a number of fair specimens. Frequently these "dapples" have the "wall" or "china eyes." The dachshund is what may be termed a whole coloured dog, at least this is what we have made him here since his adoption.

White as the ground colour is as objectionable in Germany as with us, but on the Continent a greater variety of colour is allowed, Herr Beckmann giving the legitimate colours, dividing them into four groups as follows :

First ; black, chocolate, light brown (red), hare pied, all with tan shadings. Secondly ; the same colour without the tan markings. Thirdly ; slate, mouse, silver grey, either whole coloured or with tan marks ; eyes, blueish or colourless (wall eyed) ; and fourthly, variegated, slate, mouse, silver grey with irregular black, chocolate or tan marks and blotches, with or without tan, and with one or two "wall eyes." Any one of these colours is as good as another in the Fatherland, but in case two dogs are of equal merit in other respects, the black and tan is to be preferred, or the dog most richly coloured and free from white.

What has been written, for the most part applies to the smooth coated dachshund as he is mostly known in this country. There are, however, other varieties with harder coats, some wire haired, some more or less silky haired. These longer coated hounds have not found much favour with us, although a few have occasionally appeared at our shows, where they have not attracted much notice ; and it seems odd that every now and then a rough or long coated puppy is produced from absolutely smooth parents. A peculiar instance of this is quoted in the *Field* of Jan. 19, 1895. The Kennel Book issued by the German Teckel-Klub (Teckel= Dächsel=Badgerhound) distinguishes three varieties of the dachshund—(*a*) the common short haired or smooth haired; (*b*) the rough haired; (*c*) the long haired, which is described as follows: " This variety of our common dachshund is probably derived from an original cross with the spaniel, but has been gradually bred into an independent species. With regard to shape, colour, and size, the points are identical with those of the common dachshund, the silky hair of the long-haired species forming the only distinction. This hair is soft and curly, and forms lengthy plumes under the throat, the lower parts of the body, and the backs of the legs. It is longest of all on the ears and on the lower surface of the tail, where it forms a regular ' flag,' like that of the setter or spaniel." The rough haired variety is represented by a dog strongly resembling a rough Irish terrier, but of course not so high on the legs. An original cross (in this case with a rough coated dog) may not unreasonably be surmised here also. On the Continent, the classes for dachshunds are arranged according to weight, but here the classification is according to colour and sex.

As to the voice or cry of the dachshund, he is not, as a rule, so free with his tongue as either the basset hound or beagle, but, of course, there are exceptions to this. One old hound, Mr. Harry Jones's Dina, was particularly musical in this respect, and her voice, in addition to being loud, was beautifully deep and mellow. Her daughter Juliet, though equally free, had a much less pleasant note.

There is no doubt that where dachshunds have been entered to work with terriers and used for the duties usually ascribed to a terrier, they are inclined to hunt with less music than if used as a pack or worked in connection with basset-hounds. Indeed this is pretty much the case with all hounds, and I have known a foxhound hunt pretty nearly mute when alone, but in company with his pack be as free with his tongue as any other hound; a similar thing is alluded to in the article on the bloodhound at the commencement of this volume.

J. H. Snow's, Philadelphia, Pa.
FRITZ.

THE HOUND (DACHSHUND).

ORIGIN.—The origin of this dog is lost in antiquity. A dog resembling it very closely is to be found on the monument of Thothmes III., 2000 B.C. The modern dog is essentially German.

USES.—Hunting rabbits and hares, tracking wounded animals and badgers.

* SCALE OF POINTS, ETC.

	Value.			Value.
Head and skull . . .	12	Chest		7
Jaw	5	Skin and coat . . .		13
Legs and feet . . .	20	Stern		5
Loins	8	Color		4
Body	8½			
Symmetry and quality . .	11	Total . . .		100
Ears	6½			

HEAD AND SKULL.—Long, level, narrow; peak well developed; no stop. Eyes intelligent and rather small; follow body in color. Ears long, broad, soft, set on low and well back, carried close to head. Jaws strong, level, square to the muzzle; canines recurvant.

68

CHEST.—Deep, narrow; breast-bone prominent.

LEGS AND FEET.—Fore legs very short, strong in bone, well crooked, not standing over; elbows well muscled, neither in nor out; feet large, round, strong, with thick pads and strong nails. Hind legs smaller in bone and higher; feet smaller. The dog must stand equally on all parts of the foot.

SKIN AND COAT.—Skin thick, loose, supple, and in great quantity; coat dense, short, and strong.

LOINS.—Well arched, long, and muscular.

STERN.—Long and strong, flat at root, tapering to tip; hair on under side coarse; carried low except when excited.

BODY.—Length from back of head to root of tail two and a half times height at shoulder; fore ribs well sprung; back ribs very short.

COLOR.—Any color; nose to follow body color; *much* white objectionable.

SYMMETRY AND QUALITY.—The dachshund should be long, low, and graceful, not cloddy.

WEIGHT.—Dogs, 21 pounds; bitches, 18 pounds.

THE DACHSHUND

Origin.—The origin of this dog is lost in antiquity. A dog resembling it very closely is to be found on the monument of Thotmes III, 2000 B. C. The modern dog is essentially German.

Uses.—Hunting rabbits and hares, tracking wounded animals and badgers.

*STANDARD.

General Appearance.—Long, low and graceful, not cloddy.

Head.—Wedge-shaped, long and lean, broadest at its base; skull should be moderately arched; bridge of nose somewhat curved or nearly straight, no stop; muzzle strong, not snipey, but fairly pointed, with open nostrils.

Ears.—Medium long, broad and soft, round at end, set on broad, high and well back, the inner seam carried close to the head; no folds. Ears are extremely active while the dog is on the alert.

Eyes.—Medium small, showing no white, clear and with keen expression. Jaws strong and level; teeth very strong and regular, incisors fitting close together, not overshot; canines exceedingly strong. A rubbing set of incisors is permissible.

Neck and Shoulders.—Neck long, seen from above, broad and strong, not suddenly set off from the shoulders, but tapering from the shoulders to the head; seen from the side, the neck is slightly arched. Skin of neck loose, without forming a dewlap. Shoulders well muscled and plastic.

Chest.—Deep and broad, breast-bone well developed.

Body.—Back long and moderately arched over loins, fore-ribs well sprung, back-ribs very short.

Stern.—Of medium length, strong at the root, well tapering toward the end and carried almost horizontally; hair on under side coarser, without forming a brush.

Legs and Feet.—Fore-legs very short and stronger in bone than hind-legs. Elbows with plastic muscles, not turning either in nor out. Fore-arms slightly crooked; feet large, round and strong, with thick pads and strong, large nails, toes closed and turning outward. When seen from the side fore-legs are straight, not hanging over in the knees (knuckling); hind-legs smaller in bone and higher than fore-legs; lower thigh very short and forming nearly a right angle with the upper thigh, so that the part from the hock down stands almost perpendicularly. Feet of hind-legs smaller than those of the fore-legs.

Mr. R. Koenigsbauer's (1014 So. 12th St., Philadelphia, Pa.)
" BEA FORST "

Coat and Skin.—Coat short, except on wire hairs, dense, strong and glossy, covering all parts of the body. On the leathers, very short and fine; on underside of body, stronger than on the other parts of the body. Skin, loose and supple.

Color.—Red in all tints, black and tan, liver and tan, grey and tan, and spotted tigers in which indistinctness of color is preferable to distinct spots. White markings objectionable, except a small stripe from breast-bone down. Color of nose and nails black in reds, sometimes brown or red, though black nose and nails are preferred. A dark eye is also preferred to a yellow eye in reds.

71

Weasel or cripple-like appearance, too high from the ground or too creeping. Skull too broad or too narrow, or too much arched. Ears set on too high or too low, heavy or short, too long or too narrow, or void of activity. A stop; goggle-eyes; short or dish-faced muzzle; too much lip or the reverse. Pig-jawed; bad teeth; short or thick neck; dewlap; crippled fore-arm, knuckling over in knee; lacking muscle; hare or open feet; sway back; roach-back; and weakness in loin. Flat ribs or not enough ribbing; hind-hand higher than fore-hand; keel-breast or chicken-breast; tucked-up like a greyhound; lacking muscular development of hind-quarters; cow-hocked. Stern set on or carried too high; rat-tail or brush; coarse coat or nakedness. Color lacking distinctiveness, except in wires or tigers, or too much broken hair; too much tan in black and tans, especially extending on the ears.

[*]SCALE OF POINTS.

Head and skull	12	Ears	6½
Jaw	5	Chest	7
Legs and feet	20	Skin and coat	13
Loin	8	Stern	5
Body	8½	Color	4
Symmetry and quality	11		
Total			100

COMMENTS.

The standard is so explicit in all respects, and the faults so carefully enumerated, that any further remarks would be superfluous. The scale of points as given are those adopted by the English club, though all the Dachshund clubs do not advocate "point" judging. It is simply given to show the relation of one feature to another, and should only be so considered. The occiput should not be too strongly prominent.

Mrs. Leopold Scarlet's (5 Tregunter Road, So. Kensington, London, Eng.)
"STARA 94"

ROBERT KOENIGSBAUER

BREEDER OF PURE BRED GERMAN DACHSHUNDE

1014 South 12th St.

Philadelphia, Pa.

FIESCO FORST

My stock represents the best strains of German and Austrian dogs, making it the most desirable in America. Among them are to be found the following CHAMPIONS, viz.: Champion Flott Forst, Champion Isolany Forst, Champion Racker von Jaegerhaus, Champion Hundsports Waldmann, Champion Schlupfer Euskirchen, Champion Flott Sonnenberg, Champion Dildomde Fass-An, Champion Lony Forst, and many others.

Champions Waldmann, Jaegerhaus, Euskirchen and Isolany alone have won 117 Prizes, which tells the tale.

Stud Dogs and Puppies, of the very best breeding only, to be found at my Kennels. Satisfaction guaranteed.   ROBERT KOENIGSBAUER.

From photo by Maxwell, Barnet

MR. ARTHUR O. MUDIE'S DACHSHUND WOLFERL

From photo by Maxwell, Barnet

MR. ARTHUR O. MUDIE'S DACHSHUND
SCHELM

THE DACHSHUND

BEWICK says that the Kibble-hound of his day was a cross between the old English Hound and the Beagle, which would give a low hound, but not a swift one ; indeed, lowness and swiftness are incompatible. Whether the Dachshund is a Kibble-hound, or even what a Kibble-hound exactly was, is not very clear, for kennel terms vary greatly in meaning in course of time.

The word Dachshund means " badger dog," and not " hound," as that term is used by our hunting men. He has, however, notwithstanding his use as a Terrier, many of the properties of the hound, and varietally should be classed with them ; indeed, our own native Terriers are classed with the hounds by Caius, although many of our existing varieties are of very different type from hounds. The term " Kibble-hound " may have been applied to such as were short and crooked in the leg, as if broken, and, in that sense, the Dachshund, the Basset, and some of our Dandie Dinmont Terriers, may be called Kibble-hounds.

During the last few years Dachshunds have immensely increased in numbers. It is, however, doubtful whether as regards quality and character the dog has progressed with equal steps. In fact, the Dachshund is becoming more and more a fashionable pet than a workman—a quality with which the breed was associated when it was first introduced in this country.

The following was contributed to the First Edition of this work by " Vert," whose large experience of Dachshunds entitles his opinions on the breed to be considered authoritative :—

"So much has been said and written on this breed of dogs during the few years that they have had a place in the prize schedules of our shows, that in treating the subject we shall endeavour to unsay some of the nonsense that has from time to time been put forth by some of those journals whose pages are opened to the discussion of canine matters, in one of which a certain amusing correspondent, in a playful moment, tells his readers that the ears of the Dachshund cannot be too long. Another says the body cannot be too long. Then we read that the legs cannot be too short or too crooked, with such impossible measurements as could only be found in the fertile brain of the writer. At shows we have had our special attention drawn to the veriest mongrels, and been held by the button by enthusiastic owners, and had glaring defects pointed out as characteristics of the pure breed; but, being unable to draw on our credulity to that extent, we have had to fall back on our stock of charity, and call to mind that even Solomon was young once in his lifetime. There is no breed of dogs that the English have been so tardy in taking to as the Dachshund, Satan and Feldmann being the only representatives of the breed on the Birmingham show-bench for several years; and certainly we had one judge who had the courage to grapple with this little hound when he did make an attempt to emerge from his obscurity, and we have seen the best Dachshund that has yet been exhibited passed over by a couple of 'all-round' judges of high standing at an important show, one of those Solons arguing that he was a Beagle Otter-hound, and the other that he was a Turnspit; neither of them being aware that the Turnspit was little different from a moderate crooked-legged Pug of the present time, and that it would be impossible to confine a long-backed twenty-pound dog in one of those small cages in which the little prisoner had to ply his calling. We have no wish to speculate on the early history of this breed, as, like other cases, it would be a mere leap in the dark from the same source as before alluded to. We have been seriously told that the breed came originally from France, and that once on a time, when the French army invaded Germany, and were capturing towns and provinces, the German nobles, by way of retaliation, invaded France and carried off all the Dachshunds; but as we do not find this theory supported by any authority that we have consulted, possibly the writer of the story may be entitled to the invention also.

The Dachshund is a short-coated, long-backed dog, on very short legs, of about 20lb. weight, and should not be less than 18lb., the bitches being 3lb or 4lb. less than the dogs. They must be self-coloured, although a little white on the breast or toes should not be a disqualification, as these beauty spots will crop out now and then in any breed of dogs.

The colour most in fashion just now is the fallow red and black-and-tan, but we have very good specimens of various shades of red, more or less smutty, as well as the brown with tawny markings, some of which are very handsome. In black-and-tan we do not demand pencilled toes, as in the Terrier, although, if good in every other respect, we should consider it an acquisition; but we prefer such as nearest approach the standard of excellence, and care little for shades of colour, so that it be any of those above named. The head, when of the proper type, greatly resembles that of the Bloodhound. The ears also are long and pendulous, and in a 20lb. dog should measure from $4\frac{1}{2}$in. to 5in. each, and from tip to tip over the cranium, when hanging down in their natural position, from 13in. to 14in.; the length from the eye to the end of the nose should be over 3in., $3\frac{1}{2}$in. being a good length for a dog of 20lb. weight; girth of muzzle, from 8in. to $8\frac{1}{2}$in., which should finish square, and not snipey or spigot-nosed, and the flews should be fairly developed; the eyes should be very lustrous and mild in expression, varying in colour with that of the coat; the teeth should be very strong and perfectly sound, as a dog with a diseased mouth is of little use for work, is very objectionable as a companion, and is quite unfit for the stud in this or any other breed of dogs; the neck should be rather long and very muscular. We have a brood bitch from one of the best kennels in Germany, in which the dewlap is very strongly pronounced; but this and the conical head are but rarely met with as yet. The chest should be broad, with the brisket point well up to the throat; the shoulders should be very loose, giving the chest an appearance of hanging between them; they should be well covered with muscle, with plenty of loose skin about them. The fore legs are one of the great peculiarities of the breed; these are very large in bone for the size of the dog, and very crooked, being turned out at the elbows and in at the knees; the knees, however, should not 'knuckle,' or stand forward over the ankles, as we frequently see in very crooked-legged dogs, which renders them more clumsy and less powerful. The feet should be very large, and armed with strong claws, and should be well splayed outwards, to enable him to clear his way in the burrow. Terrier-like fore feet cannot be tolerated in the Dachshund, as great speed is not required, the great essentials being: a good nose for tracking; a conformation of body that will admit of his entering the badger earth, and adapting himself to his situation; and a lion heart and power to grapple with the quarry, in the earth or in the open—and these are no small requirements. We are frequently told So-and-so's Terrier has finished his badger in some very small number of minutes. But there are badgers and badgers—baby badgers; and if we are to believe a tithe of what we hear on this head, the supposition is forced upon us that a great many badgers die in their infancy.

We do know that the premier Dachshund of the present day has drawn a wild fox from his fastness, and finished him, unaided, in about four minutes; but an unsnubbed, fully matured badger of five or six summers is an awkward customer, and with him the result might have been quite different.

What are called Dachshunds may be picked up in most

German towns; but those are often of an inferior sort, or half-breds, the genuine blue blood being almost entirely in the hands of the nobles. Familiar to us in the north were those of the late King of Hanover; those of Baron Nathasius and Baron Von Cram in the south. The Grand Duke of Baden's kennel, at Eberstein Schloss, is unrivalled. Prince Couza, Baroness Ingelheim, and Baron Haber also possessed some of the best and purest strains.

In England Her Majesty the Queen and H.S.H. Prince Edward of Saxe-Weimar for many years possessed the choicest specimens of the best strains in Germany; and we have been favoured with stud dogs and brood from some of the above-named kennels, which required something more than gold to possess them. A habit has sprung up of late—and a very bad one it is—of entering rough-coated little dogs as Dachshunds at some of our best shows, and some of them have received honours which they are in no way entitled to. This is misleading, as they are not Dachshunds, but ' Bassets '—very nice little fellows, but with no more right to be exhibited as Dachshunds than a Setter or a Spaniel would have in a Pointer class. They may be half-breds—as Dachshund-Basset or Dachshund-Spaniel. We have also met with others, hound-marked and smooth-coated, which looked like Dachshund-Beagles; these are all Bassets, a term applied by the French to all low, short-legged dogs. The best we have met with were a leash owned by a French marquis; these had grand heads of the Otter-hound type, with rough coats, very long bodies, and short, crooked legs, and were called 'Rostaing Bassets,' and were excellent workers in thick coverts; but they rarely possess either the courage or the scenting powers of the Dachshund."

Having quoted the opinions of a well-known authority in the early show days of the variety, we now give the opinions of a present-day enthusiast in the breed, Mr. Harry Jones, and one whose opinions, alike as breeder, exhibitor, and judge, are entitled to respect :—

" I do not propose in any way to deal with the ancient history of the Dachshund, but simply to write about Dachshunds as we have known them in England since they have been exhibited at our dog shows. Strange as it may appear, a separate class for this breed was given at the Crystal Palace Show in 1873, five years before the earliest record of a separate class being given for Dachshunds at a dog show in their native country—viz. at Berlin in 1878 (see Vol. I. of the 'Teckel-Stammbuch,' published by the 'Teckel-Klub' in 1891).

During the seventies the numbers of Dachshunds seen at our best shows rapidly increased, and Mr. W. Schuller, of Poland Street, imported a considerable number of the winners of the day; but the two Dachshunds, imported about this time, to whom most of the modern Dachshunds can be traced back were Waldine (6,355) and Xaverl (6,337), the former being the dam of Chenda (6,339), Hans (8,380), Zanah (8,404), etc., and the latter the sire of Hans (8,380), Zigzag (8,393), etc. etc. The latter's son Ozone (10,502) sired the two brothers Maximus (12,767) and Superbus (12,776), probably the most successful show and stud dogs of the breed in this country, but they owed a great deal of their success to their dam Thusnelda (10,528), imported by Mr. W. Schuller. She was first exhibited by Mr. Mudie at the Kennel Club Show of 1880. She was smaller than most of the Dachshunds then being shown, and was stated to have won several first prizes at Continental shows. She proved to be the most valuable importation of all the Dachshunds that passed through the hands of Mr. Schuller. Although she left no progeny in Mr. Mudie's kennel, she bred most successfully to both Ozone and Wag when in Mr. Arkwright's kennel.

There is no doubt that nearly all our Dachshunds that were too large and houndy in type obtained this from the strain of Waldine (6,355), but this strain when crossed with Thusnelda soon produced the right size and the type required.

In January, 1881, the Dachshund Club was formed, and before the end of the year a description of the Dachshund with a scale of points was published. It has often been stated that the Dachshund Club when it published the description of the variety did so in direct opposition to the acknowledged German type; but the writers who make these statements surely overlook the fact that this standard was compiled in England and published ten years before any standard or scale of points were published by any acknowledged German authority—viz. the Teckel-Klub in 1891.

The standard described the Dachshund as he was then known in this country by the imported dogs that were being exhibited, and that were stated to have won prizes before being imported, and to have been bred in the very best German kennels; but there is no doubt whatever that these imported dogs were more houndy in type than the Dachshund described in the scale of points published by the Teckel-Klub ten years later.

Although the points of the breed as published by the two clubs had important differences, there was not so much difference in the type of the dogs themselves.

In 1882 Dachshunds that were prize winners at our shows, and bred from the most successful winners of the day, competed successfully at Hanover under a German judge.

In 1885 and 1886 I exhibited Wagtail (16,633)—a daughter of Thusnelda, and the dam of Jackdaw (20,689), the most successful English-bred Dachshund ever exhibited—at the shows of the

80

St. Hubert Society, under a German judge, and each year she not only won the first prize in her class, but was awarded the *prix d'honneur* for the best Dachshund of all classes. She was a small-sized black-and-tan.

In 1891 I exhibited Pterodactyl (24,854) at Spa under a German judge, who awarded him first prize in his class, but he was not permitted to compete for the *prix d'honneur ;* and Pterodactyl was one of the most successful prize winners in England.

That Dachshunds of very different types do win prizes under our different judges is only what occurs in nearly every breed of dog ; but since the Teckel-Klub published its scale of points there has been a decided effort on the part of English breeders to breed more on the lines of the best of the German dogs, and with this object several of the winning dogs at the trials and shows have been imported during the last few years.

I think the greatest harm that is now being done to the breed in England is to change the nature of the dog, from being a hardy, keen, sporting little dog, quite able to hold his own with any dog of his size at field sports, into the ladies' pet dog we now find him. Instead of being a merry, bold, active dog in the ring, we find half of them are so shy that they cannot be induced to walk, and some will not even stand up.

That the Dachshund in his native country is a game sporting little dog will be admitted by all who have seen the trials under ground at foxes and badgers at Continental shows. Nearly all the prize winners were good workers, and some were excellent under ground.

I think it is a far more serious matter to change this sporting little companion from a hardy, courageous dog into a pet dog, nervous, delicate, and shy, than to have a difference in the scale of points."

No less interesting and practical are the opinions expressed by another well-known breeder of the variety, Mr. J. F. Sayer. That gentleman, in his review of the breed in the *Kennel Gazette* of January, 1903, states that : —

" What we want now is a few good German-bred dogs for mating with our houndy bitches to produce better stamina and courage, better legs and feet, tails, skin, and colour. The body and chest we have fairly right, and even the head, as to skull, etc., but stronger jaws are required. I have been much impressed when judging by the comparatively few Dachshunds that are really sound on their legs and able to stand evenly on their feet. Many can stand without knuckling over ; but soundness demands something more exacting than this—namely, strong (sound) feet, not too long, outspreading, and not twisted. The twisted foot is oftenest observed, and no dog with such a fault can be considered absolutely sound. Then, again, another striking fault, though not, I believe, so damning as unsoundness, is the loose shoulder—out-at-elbow— a sign of weakness in a most vital part of a Dachshund. How rarely one sees a good level back, with proper loin development! A great number of present-day winners dip behind the shoulders, and perhaps more are higher on quarters than at shoulder.

Muscle is absolutely at a discount, and its place is taken by beefiness. I wonder how many of our show dogs get more than

FIG. 55.—MISS A. M. PIGOTT'S DACHSHUND CHAMPION PRIME MINISTER.

the minimum allowance of exercise, to say nothing of work. . . . Sterns must not be neglected—curly tails, sausage tails, crooked tails, etc., are all only too apparent ; but the correct tail—not too long, strong at base, tapering gradually to the top, and moderately feathered underneath—how few do we see ! Skin of the right texture we neglect, or perhaps I should say we are losing it, in spite of ourselves, by inbreeding. The Dachshund should have plenty of thick skin, but it should be thick and covered with hair that, on being stroked the wrong way is resisting to the touch, instead of soft and yielding. Colour is rapidly fading. Red dogs are nowadays chiefly yellow, shading to whitish fawn. The beautiful cherry-red is rarely seen, and the black-and-tan is almost conspicuous on the benches on account of its unusual colour! Even the black-and-tan is losing its rich tan markings, and a lot of half-and-half colours are cropping up. Colour is certainly a minor point; but it helps to illustrate my contention that an outcross is desirable. We have long ago exploded the theory of classifying Dachshunds by colour, but there is much to be said for the care with which the Germans have preserved the colour pure. I think that we might with advantage take a leaf out of their book by classifying our dogs by weight, for the variation in size and weight of our leading winners is most extraordinary, and must be very bewildering to beginners, and even to older hands. . . . The right size and weight for a Dachshund is about 18lb. for bitches, and a couple of pounds heavier for dogs."

The practical breeder will do well to carefully digest what Mr. Sayer has written with regard to the Dachshund, for they are words of wisdom, though uttered none too soon.

Though the Dachshund (Fig. 55) in this country is not called upon, as a rule, to "work," yet occasionally we find an owner who takes a wholesome pride in those qualities that so endear the breed to its Continental admirers. We have more than once seen the working qualities of the variety put to practical test. To the fact that as a mere ornament it is of greater monetary value than as a utility animal must be ascribed the apathy exhibited by owners with regard to its working qualities; for to develop the latter to the full would be to put the dog out of court for show-bench honours. The Dachshund, taken generally, makes an ideal companion and house-guard; while it is one of the easiest of dogs to keep in first-class condition.

The matter we have quoted from Mr. J. F. Sayer's very practical contribution to the periodical above referred to sufficiently indicates the lines that the novice should go upon when selecting a dog, especially when taken in conjunction with the description of the breed furnished by the Dachshund Club and given below and the illustration that accompanies this chapter. "Vert," in his contribution at the beginning of this chaper, disapproves of the Rough-haired Dachshund; and the only addition that calls for mention in connection with the Club's description is the fact that dappled specimens are occasionally found and special classes provided for them at the larger shows.

The Dachshund standard, as settled by the Dachshund Club, November, 1881, is as follows :—

Head and Skull.—Long, level, and narrow; peak well developed; no stop; eyes intelligent and somewhat small; follow body in colour.

Ears.—Long, broad, and soft; set on low, and well back; carried close to the head.

Jaw.—Strong, level, and square to the muzzle; canines recurvent.

Chest.—Deep and narrow; breast-bone prominent.

Legs and Feet.—Fore legs very short, and strong in bone, well crooked, not standing over; elbows well clothed with muscle, neither in nor out; feet large, round, and strong, with thick pads and strong nails. Hind legs smaller in bone and higher, hind feet smaller. The dog must stand true—*i.e.* equally on all parts of the foot.

Skin and Coat.—Skin thick, loose, supple, and in great quantity; coat dense, short, and strong.

Loin.—Well arched, long, and muscular.

Stern.—Long and strong, flat at root, tapering to the tip; hair on under side coarse; carried low, except when excited. Quarters very muscular.

Body.—Length from back of head to root of stern two and a half times the height at shoulder. Fore ribs well sprung, back ribs very short.

Colour.—Any colour; nose to follow body colour; much white objectionable.

Symmetry and Quality.—The Dachshund should be long, low, and graceful, not cloddy.

Weight.—Dogs, about 21lb.; bitches, about 18lb.

SCALE OF POINTS

Head and Skull	...	...	...	...	... 12
Ears ...	...	...	...	...	... 6½
Jaw ...	...	...	...	...	... 5
Chest	...	...	...	...	... 7
Legs and Feet ...	...	...	...	...	... 20
Skin and Coat ...	...	...	...	...	... 13
Loin ...	...	...	...	...	... 8
Stern ...	...	...	...	...	... 5
Body ...	...	...	...	...	... 8½
Colour	...	...	...	...	... 4
Symmetry and Quality ...	...	...	...	...	... 11
		Total	...	...	... 100

The Dachshund Club states that it does not advocate point judging, the figures given being only used to show the comparative value of the features.

The Dachshund is one of the few varieties that can boast a Stud Book of its own. "Dachshund Pedigrees" are monumental volumes, and bear eloquent testimony to the painstaking care and research bestowed upon them by their compilers, Mr. E. S. Woodiwiss and Mr. E. Watlock Allen. They contain a list of all registered Dachshunds up to date, giving their reputed sires and dams, dates of birth, colour, breeders, owners, etc. Apart, too, from the pedigrees, there are a number of admirable reproductions in black and white of "pillars of the Stud Book," English and German dogs alike. Such a feature will be a valuable one to the breeder in the future, who will not only be able to refer to the family tree, but also to see some splendid representations of animals forming its chief branches.

84

In the volumes referred to, which should be in the possession of every one interested in the Dachshund, occur of course the names of those fanciers who have done most to place the variety upon the pinnacle of fame it now enjoys. Already some of these have been mentioned, but there are some few others who, having espoused the cause of the variety on its introduction, have retained at least their affection for it up to the present day—Mr. A. O. Mudie, Mr. A. W. Byron, Mr. Montague Wootten, Mr. E. S. Woodiwiss, Miss Pigott, Mr. W. Arkwright, Captain and Mrs. Barry, and a few others ; while the lady who at the outset was largely responsible for the dog's introduction here was Mrs. Merrick-Hoare.

To those accustomed to regard the soft-eyed, smooth-coated Dachshund as but a pampered pet-dog, incapable of little beyond the bestowal of its affection upon its owner and it may be the guarding of the house, the instructive contribution from Mr. William Carnegie ("Moorman") on the dog's working capabilities will come as a revelation. It is also to be hoped that those who have the true welfare of the breed at heart—and their name is legion—will see fit to pay attention to those workmanlike qualities that first endeared the breed to English hearts, instead of contriving to breed solely for those more ornamental ones that fickle Fashion has for the nonce ruled shall obtain :—

" The popularity of the Dachshund in this country dates now for many years back, but the curious little dogs have never achieved that position for either Terrier or Hound work that they hold in Germany, Austro-Hungary, and other parts of the Continent. They quickly secured the approval of the ' Fancy ' upon intro-duction to English kennels and the benches of our dog shows ; but to a very large, in fact, preponderating, extent their merits in field and covert, when properly trained and worked, have been either overlooked or ignored. True, there have been, and are, many owners of Dachshunds who have sought to prove their worth other-wise than as merely fancy dogs ; but whatever measure of success has crowned their efforts in this direction, the generality of those interested in the breed have not sought to follow up or extend these favourable results.

No doubt the name Dachshund, with the German translation of ' badger-dog,' has handicapped the breed for work in this country, because people naturally point to the scarcity of badgers in most parts of the British Isles, and, further, to the apparent unsuitability of the undoubtedly peculiarly built dogs for drawing badgers, their inability to tackle them, and the pronounced fact that we have numberless dogs of various Terrier breeds more suitable to work of this kind than the Dachshund itself.

It is greatly to be regretted that the breed has been so closely and so solely associated with the badger by those who patronise and stand fast by the breed. This is not the case in the Continental countries, where it chiefly predominates, and where its name has become more familiar in the semi-diminutive, semi-nicknames of Daxel or Teckel. Had the dog come to us under any other name than Dachshund, and its inevitable translation of 'badger-dog,' there would seem to be every reason to believe it would have taken better place as a worker than it has done so far.

To properly appreciate the position that the Dachshund holds in the countries that chiefly esteem it, it is necessary for the un-acquainted British amateur to compare it with the position held by some of our Terrier breeds. It is unnecessary to particularise ; but for the present purpose any popular breed of working Terrier may be taken as representative. In these islands we should have a standard of excellence which would govern the positions of the best-bred dogs at shows and elsewhere, a general type of well-bred members of the breed, and the usual mongrel riff-raff; we should have dogs bred and kept mainly for showing, others for pets or companions, and others bred and maintained solely for work in the special direction and under the special conditions demanded by various circumstances. Such is precisely the position of the Dachshund in the Continental countries named ; but it holds an additional one, possessed by no other single breed in the British Isles—it is essentially the companion of the sportsman, the woods-man, and the gamekeeper. Whatever the resources of the kennels of the one or the other, one or more Dachshunds seem to be a *sine quâ non*, and in the vast majority of cases the Daxel or Teckel will be a useful, well-trained dog, well up to any of the chance work such as a gamekeeper or a sportsman would come across in going his rounds, or in an ordinary stroll over the preserve with dog and gun.

This class of Dachshund serves as a sort of general utility dog. If a hare or a rabbit be wounded by a shot, the dog will find or retrieve it ; a varmint be found in a trap, it will kill it ; if there be fur or feather to be found and driven from covert, the dog is trained and is quite equal to the task.

These are all services such as one can command from one or other of our own breeds of dogs employed for sport ; but then a single properly trained Dachshund will perform them all, whilst the little hounds may also be trained to work more associated with their name, and which I shall describe in detail later on.

It has been made clear so far that the Dachshund is capable of work in wood, covert, or field, of no mean order, and it is now necessary to see how these faculties for work can be developed. To this end we must take some stock of the breed as we now possess it. Those who are responsible for the type of Dachshund have frequently disputed between what may be termed Hound and Terrier type, and in this respect we find one of the causes of the fallacy which the name Dachshund begets influencing judgment in the wrong direction. The Dachshund never was a Terrier in the sense that we understand it of a dog for going to ground. True, well-trained ones—trained, that is, for this particular work—will go to ground and tackle fox or badger in its earth ; but the Dachshund, as a working dog, is and must be regarded in the light of a diminutive hound, working slowly, but steadily, by scent mostly, and driving game or vermin to the gun.

There are few dogs more sure or persistent upon a cold trail or scent ; they will follow and find wounded fur and feather where smarter breeds, such as a Spaniel or a Terrier, will over-run the quarry and remain at fault ; they will also, when worked in company, follow, worry, and bring to gun or to bay far superior quarry to dogs of their own weight and size of Terrier breed.

It will therefore be seen that to promote and thoroughly bring out the working capabilities of the Dachshund, it is, to say the least, unwise to attempt to enter them upon the same lines as one would commence the education of young Terriers. It is precisely for this reason that so many failures to make good working Dachshunds have resulted.

For a portion of its work a Dachshund requires to be entered upon the same lines as the small Beagles—Beagles, that is, of about 14in., not the oversized ones, neither Beagle, Harrier, nor Hound, of 17in. to even 19in., whose size and speed are too great for one style of work and insufficient for the other. Coupled with this form of work, the Dachshund requires entering also to that portion of a sporting Terrier's work that embraces the search by scent for fur or vermin, the driving of them to gun, net, or earth, but not the actual going to earth. When Dachshunds are required to go to earth after fox or badger, whether to tackle the quarry and hold it at bay till it is dug out, or to drive it from its burrow, a specific form of training is required—upon the same lines as the low-legged Scottish Terriers are entered for work amongst the cairns and rocky grounds of our northern province where foxes are shot and caught, but not hunted with hounds.

Slow seek, sure find, is the maxim that must guide the hand that seeks to train Dachshunds to the work of which they are capable and at which they are adepts. They cannot at their best replace any of our Terrier breeds at the work at which they in their turn are *facile princeps*, but they can be brought to such a state of serviceable training in the directions which have been mentioned as will freely prove their utility and value as an addition to our list of sporting dogs. The great point is that they must receive a special course of training suited to their peculiarities of form and nature and with a due appreciation of their possible powers. Of course, the general scheme of game-preservation and woodcraft in these islands is not the same as in the far larger and wilder lands of the countries where the Dachshund is chiefly valued and used, whilst at the same time the quarry upon which they can be worked is of far more limited character and variety. At the same time, the opportunities for employing them when properly trained are many and varied, as will be seen from the experiences of their working gained in those Continental districts where they are chiefly valued, and which will be described.

To properly appreciate what well-trained Dachshunds are capable of, it is necessary to have witnessed them at work, and shared in the sport in which their services are brought to bear. Given a concise insight into the manner in which they are employed abroad—admittedly under somewhat different circumstances from those obtaining at home—the outcome of the training to which they are submitted will serve as a guide to the possibilities of their use in our own lands.

For the most part the majority of the forests and woodlands of Germany harbour many more hares than do any of our British woods and coverts ; and in districts where the Dachshund is a plentiful feature of the kennels, it is freely employed for the purpose of beating out the hares for the individual gunner, or for general beats, where several sportsmen are concerned. These woodland hares do not strike straight away when started from their forms, but display very much the same tactics as rabbits, dodging here and there amongst the undergrowth where such exists, and confining their course to lesser and more circling limits where the woods are clear and the view of the quarry is more extended.

Under these conditions the work of the Dachshund upon hares resembles very much that of a steady, slow Spaniel—less bustling and headstrong, and running more by scent than sight when once the quarry is sighted. Along drives and paths Dachshunds learn to work the ground on either side, never going deep into cover, but driving the hares to the open ground, where opportunity for shooting is greater. Many Dachshunds trained to this work will follow and retrieve a wounded hare—wounded heavily, that is, for it stands to reason that a Dachshund's pace would not be equal to running down one only slightly touched—within reasonable limits of time. Still, for all that, these dogs, when keen and thoroughly trained, are quite capable of such work, and many instances of their powers in this direction have come under my personal notice.

From the humane point of view this is a distinct merit, for the Dachshund is powerfully mawed, and makes no great fuss of cleanly killing a wounded hare and bringing it to bag. Of course we could find very little occasion for employing this breed for similar purposes in this country; but in connection with that form of sport known as hedge-popping, Dachshunds would serve wonderfully well if properly trained to the work, and would probably furnish better sport than many of the Terriers and Spaniels usually brought into this style of work, frequently to their detriment for that of a more legitimate description.

Naturally chief interest in the Dachshund and its work must centre upon what dogs of the breed can do in connection with the badger. To rightly appreciate the working of any dog on badgers, it must be borne in mind that it must be specially entered for tackling or driving out these vermin. None of our British breeds is in itself specially constituted for this work; but individual members, possessing the natural ability and disposition, figure prominently for the purpose. In just the same way, many Dachshunds are specially entered and worked upon badgers. These animals are very plentiful in many districts of Germany, but are wonderfully so upon some of the Hungarian slopes of the Carpathian Mountains. Properly trained Dachshunds are employed to hunt them to their lairs, as well as to go to earth, and either hold them in their burrows or drive them from them, when they are taken alive or shot, as the case may be.

Without going into details of the badger's merits or failings as an object of sport, or enlarging upon the details of the subject, it must, however, be pointed out that the habits of the brock are mainly nocturnal; consequently the services of Dachshunds in this respect must be attuned to the nature of the work required. The badger, seemingly a clumsy animal, can, however, go at a comparatively speaking great rate; it follows, therefore, that any dog capable of dealing with it in the open must not only possess a certain turn of speed, but be able to cope with the varmint if it comes up with it, or if the latter should turn upon its pursuer. These conditions the Dachshund is freely capable of fulfilling, and to far better advantage than the more speedy Terriers, whilst being at the same time better provided for tackling them, if it come to such necessity.

In those particular parts of the Carpathians to which reference has been made, the lower fringe of forest-land abuts right on to the higher slopes of cultivated land, where maize is largely grown. The badgers, which are remarkably numerous in these woods, are also bad enemies of the growing maize-crop, and will commit very serious depredations amongst it just before the time of harvest. The badgers will find their way down from their haunts at dusk, and, getting amongst the maize, pursue quite a devastating course. The expanses of growing corn are at times very considerable, and to deal successfully with the vermin—for such they are—many Dachshunds are employed. The routine is to put the dogs in upon them, and the men with the guns—proprietors, foresters, or watchers, as the case may be—take up positions between the growing crops and the woodland ; and as the dogs drive the badgers out, and the latter seek to reach their proper haunts, some are shot, and some are collared and killed by the Dachshunds.

It is found that no variety of dog is nearly so successful in this work as the Dachshund. His manner of working upon the badgers —chiefly by scent and sound—amongst the strong stalks of the maize is exactly that which seems most effective in getting them out and bringing them into the open ground, where they can be satisfactorily dealt with. There is a considerable element of sport and excitement about the whole business ; and although it is not unusual for an occasional dog to get severely mauled, still, as a general rule the dogs have the best of it, and the procedure indicated is found to be the most effective to employ in dealing with the circumstances described. It is obvious that the counterpart of this form of work for the Dachshund exists to only very small extent in Great Britain ; but there are certain districts where badgers are still fairly plentiful, and where a certain recognised form of sport is obtained in hunting them upon similar lines at night-time. As a rule, however, the badgers are either taken alive, or simply hunted back to their earths.

I believe I am correct in stating that a few years back a small pack of Dachshunds were successfully worked in connection with badger-hunting of this description ; and it is perfectly certain that some of the small hounds, properly entered and trained to this work, would show more extended and better sport than would Terriers employed for the same purpose. At the same time, if required to go to ground, the Dachshund is far superior for the work to Terriers of either large or small breed : the former are too heavy and upstanding for work on badgers below ground, and the smaller ones, be the individual members never so plucky or hard, not by nature suited for dealing with such a foe. The badger is in many ways a naturally inoffensive creature, and from the humane standpoint, if it be necessary to draw or kill it, it is surely preferable to adopt the speediest and least cruel manner of so doing.

Those who know the Dachshund best would never seek to place its work upon rabbits in front of that of either Terriers or Spaniels, except as a mere set-off against or as a comparison with the work of these breeds. It is true enough that under certain conditions the Dachshund would prove superior ; but these conditions are exceptional, and the colour of the breed is against it when working upon fur in close cover.

As furnishing an insight to the extreme possibilities of these little dogs, it may be mentioned that a well-known sportsman of my acquaintance, very keen on deer and ibex shooting in high grounds, has a couple of Dachshunds that he employs upon his stalks for tracking wounded quarry. He has found them to work with the greatest sureness upon comparatively cold scent, and save him many a head which otherwise might never have been brought to bag.

In conclusion, it may be remarked that the proper entering and training of Dachshunds to any of the work of which they are capable is a quite easy proceeding. They are extremely intelligent, and probably the least nervous, as a breed, of any dogs employed for similar purposes. The main point is to observe that they are not Terriers ; that the course of entering them to any quarry must be upon nearly the same lines as are adapted to the entering of Beagles or other small hounds ; that it is only sure and steady, but not necessarily slow, work of which they are capable. With these reservations, there is no reason why great numbers of the Dachshunds now existing in this country should not become as useful members of our kennels as are their congeners in Continental countries.

The Dachshund

 LIKE many other varieties of the dog, the origin of the Dachshund seems to be involved in obscurity, though there are fairly reasonable grounds for concluding that the home of the Dachshund is Germany, where the terrier-like type is that cultivated, the Hound characteristics of the breed having become largely developed through the English system of breeding.

To anyone unacquainted with this breed of dog in his own country, the Hound features are the most striking, in fact, so overshadow anything of the Terrier element as to completely obscure it.

Some few years since the Dachshund was an exceedingly fashionable variety of dog, chiefly as a lady's companion.

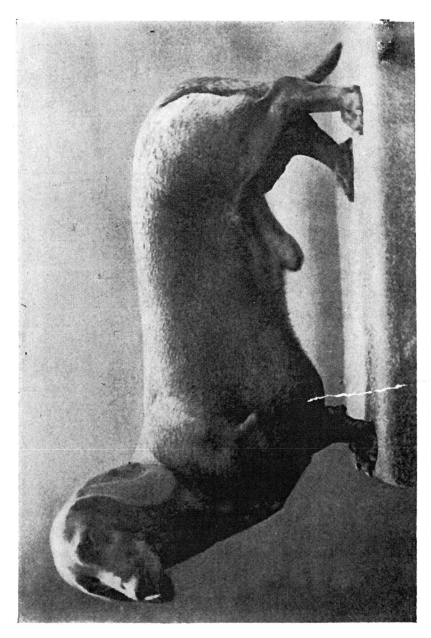

DACHSHUND CHAMPION SNAKES PRINCE Property of Mr de BOINVILLE).

93

A Brace of Typical Dachshunds (Property of Mr de Boinville).

DACHSHUND DOG AND BITCH (Property of Mrs GERALD SPENCER).

RED DACHSHUND VICTORIA REGINA (Property of Miss BLACKOE).

96

Latterly he seems to have been displaced by the Pomeranian, Pekinese, and Japanese Spaniels. This brings us back to the adage that "every dog has his day." So with the Dachshund, yet the classes at the London shows are always well filled. The Terrier-type of Hound is usually smaller and built upon lighter lines. The legs are not so crooked, the head shorter, so are the ears.

In weight they are from 10 to 16 lbs. or thereabout.

The so-called Toy Dachshund or Spiel Dachs are a diminutive production of the smallest Terrier-type of the variety, but not specially sought after, at least in this country.

In England Dachshunds are but rarely used for sporting purposes, but in Germany they are largely employed for hunting the fox in his home.

These little dogs can go into the earth after any fox, and are not long in giving tongue when Reynard is in the ground, and if several of these little dogs are at work on one fox they are not long in causing him to bolt, or settle the dispute by underground combat. With the badger—always a formidable antagonist—these little dogs are said to be equally game, usually fighting to a finish. A few sportsmen have made use of Dachshunds for driving rabbits out of cover, but they have no particular qualification in this respect, and are decidedly inferior to the Beagle, or a pack of Beagles for this purpose.

It is a variety of dog not the easiest to rear, distemper being, as in most other breeds, accountable for the high mortality amongst them.

The colour of Dachshunds varies considerably, but the chief ones are, deep red, chocolate and tan, fallow-red, black-and-tan, and dapple.

White on the body is objectionable, less so on the feet.

The so-called "Tiger Dachs," or steel-blue and tan-colour is uncommon, though it gives the animal a very handsome appearance. At the London Kennel Club shows there is a class for dappled dogs and bitches. As a rule, the crossing of a black-and-tan Dachs with a red one, produces puppies true to type, i.e., some are black and tan, others red, and not a mixture of these two colours. A red dog and bitch, will, however, sometimes throw a black-and-tan puppy; or a black-and-tan sire and dam produce a whole-red puppy. This is precisely what happens with certain other varieties.

There are really three varieties of coat, viz.:—

 (a) The Smooth.
 (b) The Rough.
 (c) Wire-haired.

The coat should be short and thick and the skin remarkably loose—a characteristic feature of the breed, and one that undoubtedly affords the animal a degree of protection during combat.

Head.—This is distinctly wedge-shaped and large in proportion to the size of the animal. Jaws strong.

Nose.—Black or Dudley (flesh) coloured. A red dog may have a black nose.

Eyes.—Well apart, with brown or black iris.

Ears.—These ought to be long, thin, covered by silky short hair and free from scales.

Neck.—Short and thick.

Chest.—Wide and deep, almost touching ground.

Shoulders.—The shoulders are very prominent and heavily clad with muscle, giving the dog a square appearance in front. A long body and well-rounded ribs are essentials.

Legs, Feet and Toes.—Most important. The fore-arm should be short and thick, running inwards so as to form almost right angles with the parts below. At the wrists or knees the parts touch each other and almost immediately bend outwards (splay-feet). as long, flat paws. These latter ought to be large and shovel-shaped, bearing long, strong, slightly-hooked claws of a black or brown colour, a white claw (as in Pugs) being objectionable. The more the "crook" the better. This, with well-rounded ribs and a long body, constitutes one of the chief points in a Dachshund, giving it a well-let-down appearance, but not too low.

Hind-quarters.—Strength in this region is of great

portance, the croup being well-rounded and the thighs strong. The loins must be well arched. The tail thick and tapering, and carried like that of the Foxhound under excitement. It must not curl over the back, this being one of the worst faults a Dachshund can have.

From 17 to 22 lbs. is the average weight of dogs in fair condition.

The Dachshund Club, and the Northern Dachshund Association, are the two principal societies, in this country, presiding over the interests of the breed.

The service of A1 stud dogs can be had at fees from two to four guineas, and excellent youngsters obtained from three to ten or twelve guineas.

The Dachshund

HE dachshund is the only dog classified as a sporting dog by the American Kennel Club which is neither a hound nor a dog exclusively used with the gun. That it is used occasionally as a hound in the sense that it follows rabbits and hares by scent as does a beagle, does not alter the fact that it is essentially a dog that goes to earth and is therefore a terrier. Its name of badger dog is all the evidence needed on that point, and that it can be made use of as a beagle does not alter the fact that it is properly an earth dog, any more than the occasional use of fox terriers for rabbit coursing makes them whippets. They are now recognized as essentially a dog of Germany, although there can be no doubt that they were found throughout Western Europe at an early date. The description of the French dogs, given in the old French sporting books copied by early English writers as applying to English terriers, leaves no doubt as to the dachshund being then a dog known and used in France. It is very true that they were called bassets, but what we know as bassets could not have gone to earth, and the name was at that time merely indicative of their being low dogs, though it must be admitted that the name was also applied to the taller, rough dog. Apparently the French gave up the small, smooth, crooked-legged dog, and it remained for the Germans to continue his use and develop him into the teckel, or dachshund, whose peculiar formation has turned many a penny for the comic newspaper illustrator.

Notwithstanding the distinctly German origin of the modern dachshund, it is due to the English fanciers to state that they were the pioneers in giving the dog the distinction of a specialty club, for as early as 1881 there was a dachshund club in England, and that was not established until the breed had been recognised for eight years as entitled to individual classification. The Crystal Palace show of 1873, not Birmingham in 1872, as given by Mr. Marples in "Show dogs," was the first to give a class for the breed which, from 1866 up to that time, had been included in the class for foreign sporting dogs. Later, in 1873, Birmingham followed the Kennel Club lead and gave its first class for dachshunds. The meaning of the German word "hund" not being so well known as it should have been in England, led to the breed being given a class in the stud book of 1874, under the title of "Dachshunds (or German Badger Hounds)," in place of badger dogs, and this led to their being considered hounds and bred for hound heads in place of the correct terrier type. Indeed, it was not until the winter of 1883-84 that Mr. George Krehl, returning from a visit to Germany, took up the question of type and led the change to that of the German dog. We were in England in December and well recollect his talk on the subject and his saying that they had been all wrong in England, but he doubted whether it would be possible to affect the change which he intended advocating in *The Stockkeeper,* which he then edited.

Doubtless the dachshund had been brought to America in the early '70's, but we think the first systematic importation of the dog for use in the field was made by Dr. Twadell, of Philadelphia, who got them for rabbiting, and there was a good deal of discussion as to their merits as compared with the longer legged beagles. Dr. Downey, of Newmarket, Md., and Mr. Seitner, of Dayton, O., then took them up, and we have always been of the opinion that the "bench-legged beagles" of Delaware and Maryland had their origin in crosses with these early importations of beagles. There use as field dogs soon died out in favour of the beagle, and after that they must be regarded as show dogs, even admitting that they are favourite dogs with many Germans who go afield after rabbits with their Waldmans and Gretchens.

Whether it is that Dr. Motschenbacker, of New York, has such a very strong kennel that he has but one opponent of any consequence, we cannot say, but on his shoulders, and those of Mr. and Mrs. Kellar, has fallen the duty of upholding the breed, so far as the Eastern shows are concerned, and it is seldom that any other exhibitor gets in ahead of these exhibitors, who have done wonders in breeding and showing winners from their own kennels.

The one exception in the East is Mr. R. Murray Bohlen, who has kept dachshunds for a good many years and the puppies he recently showed at the Atlantic City exhibition proved that he had some good breeding material.

The dachshund is such an exaggeration that it is much easier to show

CHAMPION HOLLYBERRY
Property of Mr. Arthur Bradbury, New Brighton, Cheshire, England

DELVES LADY
Winner of thirty-three firsts and specials and two firsts in championship class.
Bred and owned by Mrs. Gerald Spencer, Lewes, England

CHAMPION WIRRAL HOLLYBRANCH
Property of Mr. Arthur Bradbury, New Brighton, Cheshire, England

103

by reproductions of photographs what the best dogs look like, than to convey a clear impression to any person who has never seen one. His one distinct peculiarity is also that of the basset, the crooked forelegs, which is nothing but a deformity now scientifically bred. That this deformed foreleg is of any practical use in digging underground, we cannot believe. Perhaps we should say that its being better than the short, straight leg of the terriers which go to ground is not our opinion, and we put that idea away with the old-time belief that the loose dewclaw of the St. Bernard helped the dog to walk in, or on, the snow. At the present day, it appears from some recent remarks of Mr. Marples, that there is an attempt at doing away, in a great measure, with the dachshund front by English breeders. He writes as follows: "In these later days, there has been a tendency in England to moderate the crook of the dachshund . . . I cannot, however, go so far in the craze for sound fronts as to accept a straight-legged dachshund, as some judges do." In this, Mr. Marples is quite correct, for it is purely a fancy breed, and whether these fronts are deformities, or not, does not matter, usage and standards have made them properties of the dachshund, and it is just as easy to breed sound fronts as straight fronts; that is, legs that are properly crooked, so that the dog stands true on his feet and does not "run over," as a man does who fails to put his foot down squarely as he walks. We recognise it as a part of the breed, while we dissent from the claim that it is essentially useful in digging underground.

The German standard goes to great length in describing the dachshund, indulging in technicalities and minuteness of detail such as we find in no English standard. There seems also to be considerable difficulty in getting a good translation into language common to dog standards. The combination of a dog man who thoroughly understands German and has an equally good English education, does not seem to have been secured for the translation of this standard. The English long have had a short, clearly written standard, but it differs in several points from the German code, and, as the latter is the one in use here, that alone will be of service. We have seen three translations, and the one which seems clearest to the English reader is the one we give. It is better in its divisions into paragraphs, and clearer in its phraseology. The best part of the German standard is the illustrations, which show the ideal, and the faulty, conformation.

General Appearance.—Dwarfed, short-legged, elongated, but stiff figure, muscular. Notwithstanding the short limbs and long body, neither appearing stunted, awkward, incapable of movement, nor yet lean and weasel-like; with pert, saucy pose of the head and intelligent expression.

Head.—Elongated, and, as seen from above and from the side, tapering toward the point of the nose, sharply outlined and finely modelled, particularly in profile.

Skull.—Neither too wide nor too narrow, only slightly arched, and running gradually without break (stop) (the less the break (stop) the better the type), into a well-defined and slightly arched nasal bone.

Eyes.—Medium sized, oval, set obliquely, clear and energetical expression. Except the silver colour of the grey and spotted dogs and the yellow eyes of the brown dogs, the colour is a transparent brown.

Nose.—Point and root long and slender, very finely formed.

Lips.—Tightly stretched, well covering the lower jaw, neither deep nor snipy, with corner of mouth slightly marked.

Jaws.—Capable of opening wide, extending to behind the eyes.

Teeth.—Well-developed, particularly the corner teeth; these latter fitting exactly. Incisors fitting each other, or the inner side of the upper incisors touching the outer side of the lower.

Ears.—Relatively well back, high, and well set on, with forward edge lying close to the cheeks; very broad and long, beautifully rounded (not narrow, pointed, or folded), very mobile, as in all intelligent dogs; when at attention, the back of the ear directed forward and upward.

Neck.—Sufficiently long, muscular, lean, no dewlap, slightly arched in the nape, running in graceful lines between the shoulders, usually carried high and forward.

Shoulders.—Long, broad, and set sloping, lying firmly on fully developed thorax; muscles hard and plastic.

Chest.—Corresponding with his work underground, muscular, compact; the region of chest and shoulders deep, long, and wide; breast bone, strong and so prominent as to show a hollow on each side.

Back.—In the case of sloping shoulders and hind quarters, short and firm; if steep (straight) shoulders and hind quarters, long and weak; line of

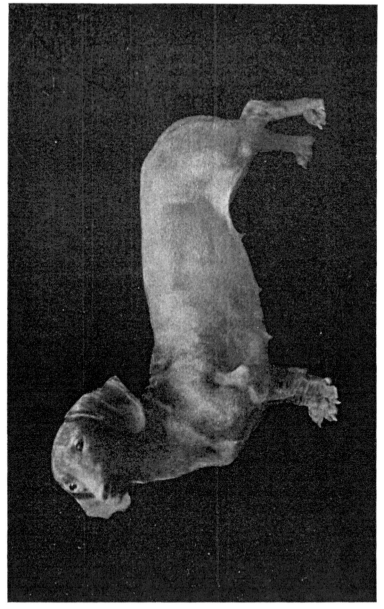

CHAMPION JANET

A prominent winner about 1900. Exhibited by Mr. E. A. Manice, Pittsfield, Mass.

CHAMPION PARSIFAL
Property of Mr. and Mrs. Karl A. Keller, Wellesley, Mass.

CH. YOUNG PHŒNOMEN, Jr.
Property of Dr. C. Motschenbacher, New York

CH. SMARTY WALDINE
Property of Mr. S. K. Gibson, Lowell, Mass.

HANNAH M.
Property of Dr. C. Motschenbacher, New York

HANSEL VON LICHTENSTEIN
German Champion—bred and owned by F. M. Widmann, Nuremberg.   Mr. Muss Arnolt, to whom we are indebted for the loan of these photographs, thus describes Hansel: "He is the soundest, lowest and longest dog I know of. He has bone, true shoulders, perfect feet and a non-faddist head. Money has never been able to buy him.

107

back behind shoulders only slightly sunk and only slightly arched near the loins.

Trunk.—Ribs full, oval, with ample width for heart and lungs, deep and hanging low between forelegs, well sprung out toward loins, loins short and tight and broad, line of.belly moderately drawn up, and joined to hind quarters with loosely stretched skin.

Hind Quarters.—Rump round, full, broad, muscles hard and plastic; pelvis bone not too short, broad and strongly developed, set moderately sloping.

Fore Legs.—Upper arm of equal length with, and at right angles to, shoulders, strong-boned and well muscled, lying close to ribs, but moving freely up to shoulder blade. Lower arm short, as compared with other animals, slightly inclined inward; strongly muscled and plastic toward front and outside, inside and back parts stretched by hard tendons.

Hind Legs.—Thigh bone strong, of good length, and joined to pelvis at right angles; thighs strong and with hard muscles; buttocks well rounded out; knee joint developed in length; lower leg short in comparison with other animals, at right angles to thigh bone, and firmly muscled; ankle bones well apart, with strong, well-sprung heel and broad Achilles tendons.

Feet.—Fore feet broad and sloping outward; hind feet smaller and narrower; toes always close together, with distinct bend in each toe; nails strong and regularly pointed outward; thick soles.

Tail.—Set on at medium height and firmly; not too long, tapering without too great curvature, not carried too high, well (but not too much) haired. (A brush tail is, however, better than one without, or with too little, hair; for to breed a weather-proof coat must always be the aim.)

Coat.—Short, thick as possible, glossy, greasy (not harsh and dry), equall ycovering entire body (never showing bare spots).

Colour.—(a) Single-coloured: Red, yellowish-red, yellow or red or yellow with black points; but one colour only is preferable, and red is better than yellowish red, and yellow. White is also allowed. Nose and nails black, red also permitted, but not desirable.

(b) Two-coloured: Deep black, or brown, or grey, each with yellow or reddish brown spots over the eyes, on the sides of the jaws and lower lips, on the inner rim of ear, on the breast, on the inside and back of legs, under the tail, and from there down one third to one half of the under side of the tail.

108

Nose and nails black in black dogs, brown in brown dogs, grey in grey dogs, and also flesh colour.

In one and two-coloured dogs, white is permissible, but only to the smallest possible extent, as spot or small streaks on breast.

(c) Spotted: Ground is a shining silver grey, or even white with dark, irregular spots (large spots are undesirable), of dark grey, brown, yellowish red, or black.

Neither the light nor the dark colours should predominate. The main factor is such a general appearance that, at some distance, the dog shall show an indefinite and varied colour which renders him particularly useful as a hunting dog. The russet-brown marks are darker in darker-spotted dogs, and yellower in the lighter ones, and there may be an indication of these in the case of a white foundation. Light eyes are permitted; when the ground colour is white, a flesh-coloured or spotted nose is not a fault. White marks are not desirable in dark dogs, but are not to be regarded as faults which disqualify.

Height at Shoulder.—7⅛ to 8⅝ inches.

Weight.—Divided into three classes: Light-weight: Dog under 16½ lbs.; bitches under 15½ lbs. Medium-weight: Dogs from 16½ to 22 lbs.; bitches, 15½ to 22 lbs. Heavy-weight: Dogs and bitches over 22 lbs.

Defects.—Too weak or crippled, too high or too low on legs; skull too wide, too narrow, or too much arched; ears set on too high, too heavy, or too short; also set on too low and narrow, or long or slack; stop too pronounced and goggle-eyes; nasal bone too short or pressed in; lips too pointed or too deep; over-shot; short, developed neck; fore legs badly developed, twisted, or poorly muscled, hare-footed or flat-spread toes; too deeply sunk behind shoulders, i. e., hollow-backed; loins too much arched and weak; ribs too flat or too short; rump higher than shoulders; chest too short or too flat; loins arched like a greyhound; hind quarters too narrow and poor in muscle; cow-hocked; tail set on high, and carried too high or too much curled; too thin, long, or hairless (rat-tailed); coat too thick, too coarse, too fine, or too thin; colour dead, dull, or too much mixed. In black dogs with russet-brown marks (tan), these latter should not extend too far, particularly on the ears.

THE DACHSHUND.

BY JOHN F. SAYER.

" Six years ago I brought him down,
A baby dog from London Town;
Round his small throat of black and brown
A ribbon blue,
And vouched by glorious renown
A Dachshund true."

—MATTHEW ARNOLD.

PERSONS unfamiliar with the sporting properties of this long-bodied breed are apt to refer smilingly to the Dachshund as " the dog that is sold by the yard," and few even of those who know him give credit to the debonair little fellow for the grim work which he is intended to perform in doing battle with the vicious badger in its lair. Dachshund means " badger dog," and it is a title fairly and squarely earned in his native Germany.

Good things are said to be done up in small parcels, and the saying is eminently true of the little dog under notice. Whether he be kept for sport or merely as a companion, he is to my mind the best dog of his size. Given proper training, he will perform the duties of several sporting breeds rolled into one. Possessing a wonderful nose, combined with remarkable steadiness, his kind will work out the coldest scent, and once fairly on the line they will give plenty of music and get over the ground at a pace almost incredible. Dachshunds hunt well in a pack, and, though it is not their recognised vocation, they can be successfully used on hare, on fox, and any form of vermin that wears a furry coat. But his legitimate work is directed against the badger, in locating the brock under ground, worrying and driving him into his innermost earth, and there holding him until dug out. It is no part of his calling to come to close grips, though that often happens in the confined space in which he has to work. In this position a badger with his powerful

110

claws digs with such energy and skill as rapidly to bury himself, and the Dachshund needs to be provided with such apparatus as will permit him to clear his way and keep in touch with his formidable quarry. The badger is also hunted by Dachshunds above ground, usually in the mountainous parts of Germany, and in the growing crops of maize, on the lower slopes, where the vermin work terrible havoc in the evening. In this case the badger is rounded up and driven by the dogs up to the guns which are posted between the game and their earths. For

MR. JOHN F. SAYER'S SPOTTED DOG
BY RACKER VON DER ECKE—LIBETTE.

this sport the dog used is heavier, coarser, and of larger build, higher on the leg, and more generally houndy in appearance. Dachshunds are frequently used for deer driving, in which operation they are especially valuable, as they work slowly, and do not frighten or overrun their quarry, and can penetrate the densest undergrowth. Packs of Dachshunds may sometimes be engaged on wild boar, and, as they are web-footed and excellent swimmers, there is no doubt that their terrier qualities would make them useful assistants to the Otterhound. Apropos of their capabilities in the water it is the case that a year or two ago at Offenbach-on-Main, at some trials arranged for life-saving by dogs, a Dachshund carried off the first prize against all comers.

As a companion in the house the Dachshund has perhaps no compeer. He is a perfect gentleman ; cleanly in his habits, obedient, unobtrusive, incapable of small-ness, affectionate, very sensitive to rebuke

or to unkindness, and amusingly jealous. As a watch he is excellent, quick to detect a strange footstep, valiant to defend the threshold, and to challenge with deep voice any intruder, yet sensibly discerning his master's friends, and not annoying them with prolonged growling and grumbling as many terriers do when a stranger is admitted. Properly brought up, he is a perfectly safe and amusing companion for children, full of animal spirits, and ever ready to share in a romp, even though it be accompanied by rough and tumble play. In Germany, where he is the most popular of all dogs, large or small, he is to be found in every home, from the Emperor's palace downwards, and his quaint appearance, coupled with his entertaining personality, is daily seized upon by the comic papers to illustrate countless jokes at his expense. He is, in truth, a humorist, as George Meredith pointed out when he wrote that

"Our Islet out of Helgoland, dismissed
    From his quaint tenement, quits hates and
    loves.
There lived with us a wagging humorist
    In that hound's arch dwarf-legged on
    boxing-gloves."

The origin of the Dachshund is not very clear. Some writers have professed to trace the breed or representations of it on the monuments of the Egyptians. Some aver that it is a direct descendant of the French Basset-hound, and others that he is related to the old Turnspits—the dogs so excellent in kitchen service, of whom Dr. Caius wrote that " when any meat is to be roasted they go into a wheel, where they, turning about with the weight of their bodies, so diligently look to their business that no drudge nor scullion can do the feat more cunningly, whom the popular sort hereupon term Turnspits." Certainly the dog commonly used in this occupation was long of body and short of leg, very much resembling the Dachshund. It was distinct enough in type to claim the breed-name of Turnspit, and many years ago this name was applied to the Dachshund.

In all probability the Dachshund is a manufactured breed—a breed evolved from a large type of hound intermixed with a terrier to suit the special conditions involved in the pursuit and extermination of a quarry that, unchecked, was capable of seriously interfering with the cultivation of the land. He comprises in his small person the characteristics of both hound and terrier —his wonderful powers of scent, his long, pendulous ears, and, for his size, enormous bone, speak of his descent from the hound that hunts by scent. In many respects he favours the Bloodhound, and I have from time to time seen Dachshunds which, having been bred from parents carefully selected to accentuate some fancy point, have exhibited the very pronounced "peak" (occipital bone), the protruding haw of the eye, the loose dewlap and the colour markings characteristic of the Bloodhound. His small stature, iron heart, and willingness to enter the earth bespeak the terrier cross.

The Dachshund was first introduced to this country in sufficient numbers to merit notice in the early 'sixties, and, speedily attracting notice by his quaint formation and undoubted sporting instincts, soon be-

MR. ARTHUR BRADBURYS CH. HOLLYBERRY
BY BRANDESBURTON MINIMUS—CARMEN SYLVA.

came a favourite. At first appearing at shows in the "Foreign Dog" class, he quickly received a recognition of his claims to more favoured treatment, and was promoted by the Kennel Club to a special classification as a sporting dog. Since then his rise has been rapid, and he now is reckoned as one of the numerically largest breeds

exhibited. Unfortunately, however, he has been little, if ever, used for sport in the sense that applies in Germany, and this fact, coupled with years of breeding from too small a stock (or stock too nearly related)

MR. DE BOINVILLE'S CH. SNAKES PRINCE
BY WODIN—VICTORIA IVEDON.

and the insane striving after the fanciful and exaggerated points demanded by judges at dog shows, many of whom never saw a Dachshund at his legitimate work, has seriously affected his usefulness. He has deteriorated in type, lost grit and sense, too, and is often a parody of the true type of Dachshund that is to be found in his native land.

To the reader who contemplates possessing one or more Dachshunds I should like to offer a word of advice. Whether you want a dog for sport, for show, or as a companion, endeavour to get a good one—a well-bred one. To arrive at this do not buy from an advertisement on your own knowledge of the breed, but seek out an expert amateur breeder and exhibitor, and get his advice and assistance. If you intend to start a kennel for show purposes, do not buy a high-priced dog at a show, but start with a well-bred bitch, and breed your own puppies, under the guidance of the aforementioned expert. In this way, and by rearing and keeping your puppies till they are of an age to be exhibited, and at the same time carefully noting the awards at the best shows, you will speedily learn which to retain and the right type of dog to keep and breed for, and in future operations you will be able to discard inferior puppies at any earlier age. But it is a great mistake, if you intend to form a kennel for show purposes, to sell or part with your puppies too early. It is notorious with all breeds that puppies change very much as they grow. The best looking in the nest often go wrong later, and the ugly duckling turns out the best of the litter. This is especially true of Dachshunds, and it requires an expert to pick the best puppy of a litter at a month or two old, and even he may be at fault unless the puppy is exceptionally well reared.

It is not within the province of this chapter to give minute directions for rearing puppies, but I may just mention a few points for the benefit of novices.

The main point I would lay stress upon is that to rear Dachshund puppies successfully you must not overload them with fat—give them strengthening food that does not lay on flesh. Lean, raw beef, finely chopped, is an excellent food once or twice a day for the first few months, and, though this comes expensive, it pays in the end. Raw meat is supposed to cause worm troubles, but these pests are also found where meat is not given, and in any case a puppy is fortified with more strength to withstand them if fed on raw meat than otherwise, and a good dosing from time to time will be all that is necessary to keep him well and happy.

Young growing puppies must have their freedom to gambol about, and get their legs strong, and this is another point I wish to emphasise. Never keep the puppies cooped up in a small kennel run or house. If you have a fair-sized yard, give them the run of that, or even the garden, in spite of what your gardener may say—they may do a little damage to the flowers, but will assuredly do good to themselves. They love to dig in the soft borders: digging is second nature to them, and is of great importance in their development.

If you have not a garden, or if the flowers are too sacred, it is better to place your puppies as early as possible with respectable cottagers, or small farmers, especially the latter, with whom they will have entire freedom to run about, and will not be overfed. My own plan is to keep my puppies at home till they are two or three months old, and then put them out to "walk" on a farm, and leave them till they are six months old, when I pass judgment on them.

My puppy kennel has a very spacious covered-in run attached, facing south. A low brick wall twelve inches high runs all round three sides, and on this is built a double matchboarded shed. The front is entirely filled with greenhouse "lights," hinged at the top and made to open to admit air without allowing rain to enter. There are also ventilators above these and just under the roof. Inside, the floor is slightly higher than the ground outside, which slopes away. This floor was arranged in the following way:—The ground was dug out to a depth of two feet and filled in with ashes well pressed down. On top there are six inches of dry garden mould, also well pressed down, but capable of being forked over and renewed from time to time. This makes a very sanitary, warm floor for the puppies to run about on ; it never smells offensively, and it is always dry, the droppings can be easily removed, and even if left a day or two are deodorised by the earth. I also had an artificial "earth" or tunnel made in the run extending the whole length, and ending in a "den." This was constructed of boarding on the sides and top, and buried in the run to a depth of several inches. This artificial "earth" was copied from that used in Germany, where, at the dog shows, trials for Dachshunds and terriers are sometimes held on fox and badger, and my puppies find it a never-ending source of amusement. Here they play for hours, running in and out, and here every tit-bit in the shape of bones is taken, to be consumed at leisure. Great is the excitement when the fortunate possessor of a bone comes to bay in the den of this run, the other puppies charging him in rushes, fighting and scrambling and keeping up an incessant barking till either the bone is consumed or they lie down exhausted to

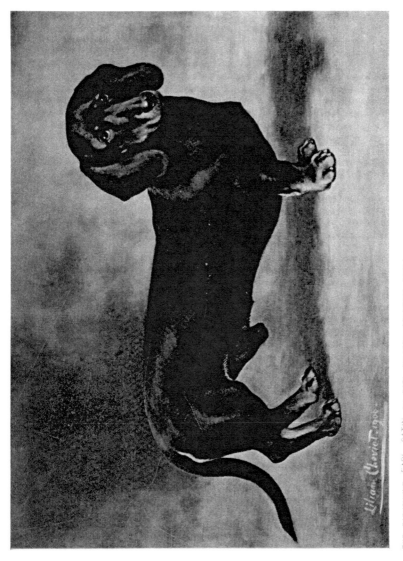

THE DACHSHUND EARL SATIN BY EARL EULER— COUNTESS TEKLA

THE PROPERTY OF MISS M. W. S. HAWKINS, HAYFORD HALL, BUCKFASTLEIGH

From the painting by Lilian Cheviot

115

dream they are engaged in mortal combat with the badger. I am sure there is nothing like keeping puppies amused in some such way—keep them on their feet as much as you can, but at the same time let them have a warm bed to retire to directly they feel tired.

Also, if you intend to show your puppies, you should begin some time in advance to school them to walk on the lead and to stand quiet when ordered to. Much depends on this in the judging ring, where a dog who is unused to being on a lead often spoils his chances of appearing at his best under the (to him) strange experiences of restraint which the lead entails.

During the past five-and-twenty years the names of two particular Dachshunds stand out head and shoulders above those of their competitors. I refer to Champions Jackdaw and Pterodactyl. Jackdaw had a wonderful record, having, during a long show career, never been beaten in his class from start to finish, and having won many valuable prizes. He was credited with being the most perfect Dachshund that had ever been seen in England, and probably as good as anything in Germany.

Ch. Jackdaw was a black and tan dog, bred and owned by Mr. Harry Jones, of Ipswich. He was sired by Ch. Charkow, out of Wagtail, and born 20th July, 1886. Through his dam he was descended from a famous bitch, Thusnelda, who was imported by Mr. Mudie in the early 'eighties. She was a winner of high honours in Hanover. The name of Jackdaw figures in all the best pedigrees of to-day.

Ch. Pterodactyl was born in 1888, and bred by Mr. Willink. He was in a measure an outcross from the standard type of the day, and his dam, whose pedigree is in dispute, was thought to have been imported. After passing through one or two hands he was purchased by Mr. Harry Jones, and in his kennel speedily made a great name in the show ring and at the stud, and was eventually sold for a high price to Mr. Sidney Woodiwiss, who at that period had the largest kennel of Dachshunds in England.

" Ptero," as he was called, was a big, light red dog, with wonderful forequarters and great muscular development. He also possessed what is called a " punishing jaw " and rather short ears, and looked a thorough " business " dog. He had an almost unbroken series of successes at shows in England, and, being taken to Germany (in the days before the quarantine regulations), he took the highest honours in the heavyweight class, and, I think, a special prize for the best Dachshund of all classes. This dog became the favourite sire of his day and the fashionable colour.

The black and tan thereupon went quite out of favour, and this fact, coupled with the reckless amount of inbreeding of red to red that has been going on since Ptero's day, accounts largely for the prevalence of light eyes, pink noses, and bad-coloured coats of the Dachshunds, as a class, to-day.

Efforts have been made by a few enthusiasts, from time to time, to stem the tide of degeneracy by importing stud dogs from Germany, and during the last few years considerable good has been done. Notable among these outcrosses was Captain Barry's Boch Bier, a middle-weight black and tan. The difference in type between this dog and our English-bred ones was most pronounced, but the reign of a more enlightened understanding was setting in, and Boch Bier's good qualities took him right to the front, and gained him the proud title of champion. He was not nearly as much used by breeders as he should have been, on account of his colour—black and tan—whereas it is to this colour that fanciers must turn to improve their washed-out " patchy " yellows, light eyes, flesh noses, and Basset-hound white markings.

Other notable importations during recent years have been Mrs. Nugent's Florian, a small red dog ; Mrs. Blackwell's Rothei Beelzebub, a heavy-weight dark red, with a long record of successes both in Germany and England, and probably the best dog ever imported ; and my own dog Racker von der Ecke, a black and tan.

The dapple Dachshunds imported by the

late Mr. George Krehl and the late Mr. Tooth, Unser Fritz, Wenzel Erdmannsheim, and Khaki Erdmannsheim, sired many useful Dachshunds, but their colour was not in vogue, and breeders hesitated to introduce

MR. CLAUDE WOODHEAD'S
CH. BRANDESBURTON MIMOSA
BY CH. SLOAN——TOSCA.

dapple blood into their kennels. Of these dapples Unser Fritz, a small dark silver dapple, was the most successful, and mated to the English-bred dapple bitch Tiger Tessie, sired some wonderful youngsters which competed and more than held their own with the other colours in the ring.

It is impossible to enumerate the hundred and one champions and famous winners that have flitted across the stage of life during twenty-five years, or are still living; but the large majority of them trace their pedigrees back to Champions Jackdaw and Pterodactyl, and an examination of the family trees of the most noted Dachshunds of to-day will show how closely they are related one to another.

A very serious aspect of the inbreeding craze is the mental deterioration involved; not only in Dachshunds, but in many other breeds of dogs kept and bred for " fancy " points, and not working qualities. In the case of Dachshunds we have lost grit and gameness to an alarming extent, and even *ordinary intelligence*, and in these respects the English dog is immeasurably the inferior of the German dog. It goes without saying that we have lost stamina too, and I was even told a short time ago by a prominent exhibitor that Dachshunds should

not be taken out to exercise on the roads because it made them go unsound ! Shade of Jackdaw, what do you think of that !

A Dachshund that cannot do a day's work on the roads when required is a travesty of what a Dachshund should be. If exercise brings out unsoundness, you must look elsewhere for the fault—to his anatomy. Inbreeding to a specified extent is resorted to, to stamp certain characteristics on a type; but it must be borne in mind that both good and bad points exist, and both may be transmitted, and whilst you may get almost perfection physically, you may at the same time reach insanity, mentally, by inbreeding.

In 1881 the prominent English breeders formed the Dachshund Club, and set about drawing up a " standard of points " as a guide for the breeding and judging of the Dachshund. At this time no similar club or standard of points existed in Germany, and our English club was therefore obliged to rely on such evidence as it could collect from individuals in Germany, no two of whom probably were in exact agreement, and on their own powers of observation coupled with that innate faculty of our

MRS. A. L. DEWAR'S RED BITCH
CH. LENCHEN
BY CH. SNAKES PRINCE——FASHODA.

race in all matters appertaining to the breeding by selection of pure stock of any animal, which has made us famous the world over, for the drawing up of what was a most important document.

A great controversy has raged for some years over this standard of points which treats the Dachshund as a "hound" pure and simple, and entirely taboos the "terrier," but at the time of its inception it was undoubtedly a useful guide for all interested in the breed.

Where I think the Dachshund Club made a great mistake was in not approaching the German Teckel Club, when it was formed some years later, and when it drew up its standard description of the points of the true type of Dachshund, and then revising the English standard to accord with the German version. The Dachshund is a German dog—practically the national dog—and the Germans should know better than we do the type best fitted for the severe work which the dog is expected to perform, and which even the German show dogs perform to-day.

Unfortunately the English club apparently made no effort to this desirable end, and it was only in the year of grace, 1907, that a select committee, appointed by the two clubs that now look after the interests of the breed, agreed to revise the English standard to bring it into line with the German. This is a step, though a late one, in the right direction, but it will take years perhaps to eradicate the evil done to the breed by the misconception of the true type.

I cannot do better than give the standard of points formulated by the Germans, which will very soon, I trust, be the standard adopted by the authorities in this country for the guidance of breeders and judges of the Dachshund.

Some illustrations of typical specimens of the breed accompany this article, and these should be studied in conjunction with the description of the points which follows. Especially I would direct attention to Ch. Snakes Prince (p. 307) as being regarded on both sides of the Channel as eminently typical. A German authority, Herr E. von Otto Kreckwitz, having seen the illustration of this dog, wrote that he "never saw a Teckel nearer to my ideal than Snakes Prince, if his weight were only 18 lb. instead of 22 lb. His perfect back, the enormous bone, deep breast, length of head, and depth; everything is complete."

There are, strictly speaking, three varieties of Dachshund—(a) the short-haired, (b) the long-haired, and (c) the rough-haired.

Of these we most usually find the first-named in this country, and they are no doubt the original stock. Of the others, though fairly numerous in Germany, very few are to be seen in this country, and although one or two have been imported the type has never seemed to appeal to exhibitors.

Both the long-haired and rough-haired varieties have no doubt been produced by crosses with other breeds, such as the Spaniel and probably the Irish Terrier, respectively.

In the long-haired variety the hair should be soft and wavy, forming lengthy plumes under the throat, lower parts of the body, and the backs of the legs, and it is longest on the under side of the tail, where it forms a regular flag like that of a Setter or Spaniel. The rough-haired variety shows strongly a terrier cross by his "varmint" expression and short ears.

The Germans also subdivide by colour, and again for show purposes by weight.

MISS M. W. S. HAWKINS' LONG-HAIRED DACHSHUND ALEXANDER SCHNAPPS
BY SCHNAPPS—ALEX.

These subdivisions are dealt with in their proper order in the standard of points, and it is only necessary to say here that all the varieties, colours, and weights are judged by the same standard except in so far as they differ in texture of coat. At the same time the Germans themselves do not regard the dapple Dachshunds as yet so fixed in type as the original coloured dogs, and this exception must also apply to the long- and the rough-haired varieties.

The following German standard of points is interspersed with my own comments and explanations :

1. General Appearance and Disposition.—In general appearance the Dachshund is a very long and low dog, with compact and well-muscled

and of a dark colour, except in the case of the liver and tan, when the eyes may be yellow ; and in the dapple, when the eyes may be light or " wall-eyed."

4. Nose.—Preferably deep black. The flesh-coloured and spotted noses are allowable only in the liver and tan and dapple varieties.

The appearance of flesh-coloured noses in the red dogs is probably produced by long-continued inbreeding, or breeding red to red from generation to generation, causing a weakness of the colouring matter in the system, and indicating partial albinoism.

5. Ears.—Set on moderately high, or, seen in profile, above the level of the eyes, well back, flat, not folded, pointed, or narrow, hanging close to the cheeks, very mobile, and when at attention carried with the back of the ear upward and outward.

6. Neck.—Moderately long, with slightly arched

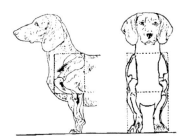

FOREQUARTERS, CORRECT.

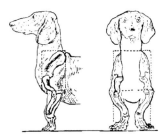

FOREQUARTERS, INCORRECT.

body, resting on short, slightly crooked forelegs. A long head and ears, with bold and defiant carriage and intelligent expression. In disposition the Dachshund is full of spirit, defiant when attacked, aggressive even to foolhardiness when attacking ; in play amusing and untiring ; by nature wilful and unheeding ; but with proper training quite as faithful, affectionate, and obedient as any other variety of dog, and with, on the whole, a well-developed intelligence.

2. Head.—Long, and appearing conical from above, and from a side view, tapering to the point of the muzzle, wedge-shaped. The skull should be broad rather than narrow, to allow plenty of brain room, slightly arched, and fairly straight, without a stop, but not deep or snipy. The jaws are capable of being widely opened, and, extending behind the eyes, set with teeth which interlock, exactly, or the inner surface of the upper incisors in contact with the outer surface of the lower set.

3. Eyes.—Medium in size, oval, and set obliquely, with very clear, sharp expression

nape, muscular and clean, showing no dewlap, and carried well up and forward.

The existence of dewlap, besides being wrong, has the effect of making the head appear short.

7. Forequarters.—His work underground demands strength and compactness, and, therefore, the chest and shoulder regions should be deep, long, and wide. If of proper formation, the forequarters govern the possession of the correct legs and feet. The shoulder blade should be long, and set on very sloping, the upper arm of equal length with, and at right angles to, the shoulder blade, strong-boned and well-muscled, and lying close to ribs, but moving freely.

The lower arm, short in comparison with other animals, is slightly bent inwards, and the feet should be turned slightly outwards, giving an appearance of " crooked " legs approximating to the cabriole legs of a Chippendale chair. Straight, narrow, short shoulders are always accompanied by straight, short, upper arms, forming an obtuse angle, badly developed brisket and " keel " or chicken breast, and the upper arm being thrown forward by the weight of the body behind causes the legs to knuckle over at the "knees." Broad, sloping shoulders, on the other hand, insure soundness of the forelegs and feet.

Unsoundness, or knuckling over of the front legs, is usually put down to constitutional weakness (and it is, of course, hereditary), or the want of, or too much, exercise, and, in fact, to every imaginable excuse, even to "carelessness"; but the fault is really due to the above-mentioned incorrect formation of the shoulder, and it is in this respect that breeders should be particularly careful in selecting for breeding purposes the most perfect bitches. Given the right shoulders, the legs and feet will be right, and unsoundness will decrease to vanishing point. Unfortunately this formation has been so little understood by our English breeders that our strains have been bred for generations from good and bad specimens indiscriminately, and with a deplorable result.

strong in bone, slightly bent inwards ; seen in profile, moderately straight and never bending forward or knuckling over. Feet large, round, and strong, with thick pads, compact and well-arched toes, nails strong and black. The dog must stand equally on all parts of the foot.

Where the feet are unduly turned out owing to incorrect formation of shoulders, the dog does not stand equally on all parts of the foot, and the feet are usually in this case weak and flat, and sometimes spreading. You can generally tell a sound dog by his compact feet.

9. Body.—Should be long and muscular, the chest very oval, rather than very narrow and deep, to allow ample room for heart and lungs, hanging low between front legs, the brisket point should be high and very prominent, the ribs well sprung out towards the loins (not flat-sided). Loins short and strong. The line of back only slightly depressed behind shoulders and only slightly arched over loins. The hindquarters

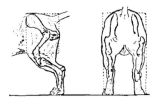
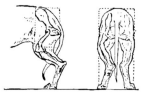

HINDQUARTERS, CORRECT.   HINDQUARTERS, INCORRECT.

It is well known to exhibitors of Dachshunds that puppies which develop quickly and get well-crooked legs at an early age invariably go unsound when they begin to "furnish up" in body —that is, when the weight of the body increases. If the shoulders are not of the correct formation an undue strain is thrown forward on to the front legs, causing them to knuckle over or turn out at the elbows.

An idea exists only too widely that, however unsound a bitch may be, she will "do for breeding from," and her puppies will come sound if the sire is sound. This is a delusion. Some may be sound, but will have inherited a defect which will soon crop up again in their descendants. Always breed from your soundest bitches, which may or may not be up to show form in other points, but which must have good understandings if you wish to establish a good sound strain. Of equal importance, at least, is it that the sire you use should also be sound, and what is quite as important, he should come from sound stock. All these things entail considerable trouble sometimes to ascertain, but haphazard breeding is fatal to ultimate success.

8. Legs and Feet.—Fore-legs very short and

should not be higher than the shoulders, thus giving a general appearance of levelness.

A very marked arch over loins is a fault, and so is a hollow back, and the latter denotes weakness.

10. Hindquarters.—The rump round, broad, and powerfully muscled ; hip bone not too short, but broad and sloping ; the upper arm, or thigh, thick, of good length, and jointed at right angles to the hip bone. The lower leg (or second thigh) is, compared with other animals, short, and is set on at right angles to the upper thigh, and is very firmly muscled. The hind legs are lighter in bone than the front ones, but very strongly muscled, with well-rounded-out buttocks, and the knee joint well developed. Seen from behind, the legs should be wide apart and straight, and not cowhocked.

As with the forequarters, a bad development, and straight, instead of sloping, position of the hip bone, affect the carriage of the hindquarters and make for weakness.

The hind feet are smaller in bone than the forefeet, and narrower.

The dog should not be higher at the quarters than at shoulder.

120

11. Stern.—Set on fairly high, strong at root, and tapering, but not too long. Neither too much curved nor carried too high ; well, but not too much, feathered ; a bushy tail is better than too little hair.

12. Coat and Skin.—Hair short and close as possible, glossy and smooth, but resistant to the touch if stroked the wrong way. The skin tough and elastic, but fitting close to the body.

13. Colour.—*One Coloured :*—There are several self colours recognised, including deep red, yellowish red, smutty red. Of these the dark, or cherry, red is preferable, and in this colour light shadings on any part of the body or head are undesirable. " Black " is rare, and is only a sport from black and tan.

Two Coloured :—Deep black, brown (liver) or grey, with golden or tan markings (spots) over the eyes at the side of the jaw and lips, inner rim of ears, the breast, inside and back of legs, the feet, and under the tail for about one-third of its length. In the above-mentioned colours white markings are objectionable. The utmost that is allowed being a small spot, or a few hairs, on the chest.

Dappled :—A silver grey to almost white foundation colour, with dark, irregular spots (small for preference) of dark grey, brown, tan, or black. The general appearance should be a bright, indefinite coloration, which is considered especially useful in a hunting dog.

Very little attention has been paid to breeding for colour in this country, and the subject is not understood ; but in Germany, where the Dachshund is classified at shows by colour as well as by weight, the breeding for colour has been brought to a fine art, and certainly, though a good dog, like a good horse, is never of a bad colour, it is good to look upon perfection of colour as well as other points. Very elaborate advice is laid down in Germany for the guidance of breeders in keeping the colours pure, and some of the colours have special clubs to promote the breeding.

Speaking generally, on this very large subject, it may be noted as an axiom that light eyes, red noses, and pale colours are produced by the too close breeding of red to red. Brown, or liver, dogs bred to red produce flesh-coloured noses and false colours—as, for instance, the pale " chocolate " and tan—and more use should be made of the black and tan to obtain the desirable black nose, eye, and rich colour, whether red or liver.

The original colour of the Dachshund was black and tan, and it is the most prominent still on the Continent, but it has been neglected for many years, and with a deplorable result as far as colour goes.

14. Weight.—Dachshunds in Germany are classified by weight as follows :—*Light-weight*—Dogs up to 16½ lb., bitches up to 15½ lb. *Middle-weight*—Dogs up to 22 lb., bitches up to 22 lb. *Heavy-weight*—Over 22 lb. *Toys*—Up to 12 lb. The German pound is one-tenth more than the English. The light-weight dog is most used for going to ground.

For the purpose of showing the comparative values of the " points," as set forth in the foregoing standard, I add the following table of values. The German club does not give this.

General appearance	.	.	.	10
Head and skull	.	.	.	9
Eyes	.	.	.	3
Ears	.	.	.	5
Jaw	.	.	.	5
Neck	.	.	.	3
Forequarters	.	.	.	10
Legs and feet	.	.	.	25
Body	.	.	.	9
Hindquarters	.	.	.	10
Stern	.	.	.	5
Coat and skin	.	.	.	3
Colour	.	.	.	3
Total	.	.	.	100

At the time of writing there are three specialist clubs to foster the breeding of true type Dachshunds in the United Kingdom. Of these one is Scottish and two are English. The English clubs are " The Dachshund Club " (Hon. Sec., Capt. Barry, 12, Queen's Gate Terrace, London, S.W.) and " The Northern Dachshund Association " (Hon. Sec., T. A. Lever, Esq., Greville Lodge, Dickenson Road, Rusholme, near Manchester). The honorary secretaries of either club will furnish all information relative to membership. " The Scottish Dachshund Club " has for its honorary secretary Mr. A. Tod, 5, St. Andrew Street, Edinburgh.

121

DACHSHUNDS.

THE Dachshund is a native of and was imported from Germany ; but by whom he was first imported or how he originated it is impossible to say. He is said to have been used, for sport, in Germany, for generations, and in that country, and other parts of the Continent, he is to-day used for finding and marking Foxes and Badgers. In this country he is kept almost solely as a house dog or for exhibition. At his own game, however, he has few equals.

The Dachshund is not a hound although occasionally used as such ; he is essentially a dog for going to earth. That he was little understood in this country when first exhibited in the "Foreign Dogs" classes is instanced by the following description of some of the earliest dogs shown. In 1870, at Birmingham, "Feldman" (2272) was described as "Pure German Badger Hound." In 1872, at the same place, "Dax" (2270) was entered as a "German Dax-hound," and Lord Onslow's "Waldmann" (2279) and "Graefin" as "German Badger Hounds." All of these dogs are described in the first three volumes of the Kennel Club Stud Book as "Dachshunds or German Badger Hounds." The dogs being so described no doubt greatly led to the hound type of Dachshunds being awarded the principal prizes at the early shows. And this type was further favoured by reason of the fact that several of the imported dogs, which had won prizes in Germany, were very houndy in type.

In 1873 classes for the breed were provided for the first time at the Crystal Palace and Birmingham Shows ; but the names of few, if any, of the winners at the quite early shows are to be found in the pedigrees of the later-day champions. There were several changes in the manner of dividing the classes at the shows. At the Kennel Club and Birmingham Shows, in 1874, the division was "Red" and "other than Red." This division the Birmingham

Show maintained until 1883. In 1884 this show abolished the division of classes by colour; but at the Kennel Club Show, in 1875, the division was "Black and Tan" and "other than Black and Tan." In 1877 a further division was made, *i.e.*, that of weight, and in 1878 that of height. But in 1879 the Kennel Club Show returned to the old order of "Black and Tan" and "other than Black and Tan"; and in 1882 all colours competed together.

To Xaverl (6,337), a red dog whelped in 1876, and imported from the Royal Kennels, near Stuttgart, and Waldine (6,355), a black and tan bitch whelped in 1874, from the Prince of Nassau's Kennels, can be traced most of the celebrated prize-winning Dachshunds in this country. Xaverl was on the light side, very active, with a deal of quality; Waldine was on the heavy side, very houndy in type and heavy in bone. Their first litter, bred by Mr. W. Arkwright, produced Hans (8,380), Senta (8,401), Zanah (8,404), and Zaidee. From each of these four, champions were bred; but each of the four had more or less white feet, which came through their dam Waldine, for Xaverl, when mated with other bitches, sired puppies free from white. And to Waldine can be traced all the oversize and very houndy type of our Dachshunds, as all subsequent out-crosses with imported dogs produced smaller and less houndy specimens.

In 1877 Major Cooper's Waldmann (7,402) was very successful, winning firsts at both the Kennel Club Show and Birmingham. This dog, bred by His Excellency Count Munster, was a black and tan of excellent type and size, quite the type of the best dogs recently seen at the important shows in Germany. It was a great loss to the breed that this dog was not available for stud purposes. In 1878 two very good Dachshunds were bred. These were the red dog Zigzag (8,393), by Xaverl ex Elsa, bred by Mr. Montague Wootten, and the black and tan dog Faust (8,379), by Dessauer (6,326), bred by Mrs. P. M.

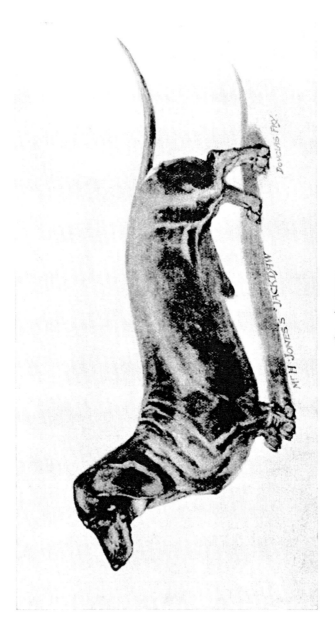

CH. JACKDAW.

MR. H. JONES'S "JACKDAW"

DOUGLAS FOX.

Hoare. Neither of these dogs was very houndy in type; each was good in chest, loin and stern and had a long, punishing head. Teck (8,389), a very good red dog, was imported from the Royal Kennels, near Stuttgart, and was very successful on the show bench, though he was not a great success as a sire. Mr. E. Hutton's Haufmann (8,381), a very nice black and tan dog, was most successful on the show bench; he had a very good head and powerful jaw, but he was too large.

In 1879 Xaverl and Zigzag were undoubtedly the best dogs being shown. In the following year, however, two Dachshunds appeared on the show bench which have played an important part in the history of the breed in this country. These were Ozone (10,502), a red dog, by Zigzag ex Zaidee, and Thusnelda (10,528), a black and tan bitch, imported from Germany, and exhibited by Mr. A. O. Mudie. The latter was a first prize winner at Hanover, Munich, Ems and Ulm. She was shown at the Kennel Club Show in June, and appeared small and light in bone when compared with such dogs as Chenda (6,339), Alma (10,510), Beckah (8,394) and Dina (6,340). But there was no doubt about her type and quality, the very things desired in an outcross. She went to Mr. Arkwright's kennel, and in her first litter to Ozone she bred, in May, 1881, Maximus (12,767), Superbus (12,776) and Mignonne (12,798). The two former were most successful on the show bench as well as at stud. The three, when first shown at the Kennel Club Show in 1882, took all before them, Maximus being first and Superbus second in dogs, and Mignonne first in bitches; she took the cup for the best Dachshund in the show. Amongst the many other good Dachshunds that Thusnelda bred was Wagtail (16,633), the dam of the celebrated Jackdaw (20,689). In 1880 Mr. Wootten bred Jezebel (10,519) and Zulette (10,534), by Zigzag ex Zanah. The former was a small chocolate coloured bitch, very good in body, loin and quarters, with the straight tapering stern

CH. JACKDAW
when 13 years old.

so much esteemed by German breeders, and quite sound. Zulette was a good coloured red, much more houndy in type, with more bone and a lot of loose skin. Both these bitches did a lot of winning and bred a number of well-known specimens.

In 1881 the Dachshund Club was formed to look after the interests of the breed, the founders being Mr. W. Arkwright, Mr. Montague Wootten, the Rev. G. F. Lovell and the present writer. The description of the breed as adopted by the Club will be found on page 474. The best Dachshund that came out in this year was undoubtedly Hagar (11,672), a black and tan bitch, by Hans ex Linda, bred by Mr. A. W. Byron and exhibited by Mr. Montague Wootten. Hagar was very good in head and jaw, and had good body and bone, and was sound. She was, however, too large. She was most successful on the show bench, and at the Kennel Club Show she took all before her, beating both Zigzag and Ozone. Rosa (11,683), litter sister to Hagar, was awarded an equal second with Zulette at this show. But the dogs were very different in type. Rosa had a long, punishing head, was rather tight in skin, a little high on the leg and not much crook; like Hagar, she had a bad carriage of stern. Zulette was inclined to be short in the face, very houndy in set on and carriage of ear, low on the leg, with a lot of crook and loose skin. At the Kennel Club Show in 1883 Mr. Arkwright brought out Lady (14,242), by Wag ex Thusnelda, Wag being by Bodo ex Olga (7,416) and Bodo by Bergmann (5,281) ex Chenda (6,339). Lady was a great success on the show bench and one of the best headed Dachshunds then being shown. She was not particularly houndy in type, her ears were set on high, and she had great length of head and very powerful jaw.

In 1884 Mr. H. A. Walker and Mrs. P. Merrik Hoare had each a very strong kennel and won most of the principal prizes. In this year three very good Dachshunds were bred, namely, Graf III. (17,554), Joubert (17,034) and Joan of Arc (17,117). Graf III. was long in the body and very short on the leg, with a long clean head, and ears not too long and well set on. Joubert and Joan of Arc were much smaller and quite of the working type ; they were active and sound, had a lot of quality and were both very successful on the show bench. Joubert had only a short career, as he died after the Aquarium Show in 1886, but he had beaten all the best dogs with the exception of his sire, Maximus, to whom he was "reserved" at this show for the best dog

KILMANOCK CORNSTALK.

exhibited. Joan of Arc had a most distinguished show career, winning the Club's Fifty Guinea Challenge Cup several times. She died after whelping in January, 1887. Her son, Jingle (24,845), was a great success as a sire. The Rev. G. F. Lovell bred a good Dachshund this year, namely, Gil Blas (17,174), by El Zingaro (10,490) ex Segesta, a good coloured red, and sound, good bone and very good body and quarters, but a little dished in face.

In 1885 Sir W. Ingram bred Indiana (19,527), a very good black and tan by Dessauer III. (14,843). This bitch had a long head and was much shorter in ear than many

129

of the winners about this time; she was very sound and had good bone. Another good bitch, Cerise II. (20,720), was shown by Mr. S. Vale, and was most successful on the show bench. She was one of the best of her time for outline of body; she was short in ear, had a very good straight stern, but was inclined to be light in bone. Neither of these bitches could be described as houndy in type, although there was a general inclination on the part of some exhibitors to breed for length of ear and a houndy expression. At the show held during this year at Brussels, Mr. Arkwright purchased Belgian Waldmann (19,525), a black and tan dog with a long, clean cut head. This dog had won at numerous shows under German judges; he was quite typical of the winners at the best German shows at the present time and sired two good Dachshunds in Belgian Herr (20,675), and Brussels Sprout (20,719). At the same show the writer exhibited Wagtail (16,633), by Wag ex Thusnelda, a small black and tan bitch, long and very low, with sound legs and feet, and a long, clean head. She not only, under a German judge, won first in her class (under 7 Kilos) but also the Prix d'honneur for the best Dachshund of all classes. This she repeated in the following year.

In 1886 Wagtail bred Jackdaw (20,689), considered by many judges to have been the best of the breed ever shown in this country. He was a black and tan, long in the body, with very good loin and quarters, short on the leg and very sound; he had a long head, but was not so wide and flat in skull as the German standard states. He continued sound in legs and feet up to his death in September, 1900. When a puppy he carried all before him in 1887 at the Kennel Club Show, winning the Fifty Guinea Challenge Cup, and he continued his unbeaten record up to the end of his show career in 1894. He won over a hundred first and special prizes, cups and medals.

Mr. Harold Blackett's Jupiter (22,660), a nice, small red

dog by Joubert, came out in 1887 and did a lot of winning. In the same year Mrs. P. M. Hoare's Sieger (22,668), another good coloured red, was a very successful winner; he was, however, very much inbred to Superbus and quite of the houndy type. Mr. Arkwright exhibited Scarsdale Jungfrau (22,696), by Joubert, a very sound Dachshund with a lot of quality.

In 1888 Pterodactyl (24,854) was first seen, at the Birmingham Show, on the show bench. This dog played an important part in the history of the Dachshund in this country. He was a good second to Jackdaw as a prize winner, and the combination of the Jackdaw and the Pterodactyl blood produced the best Dachshunds of the day. Pterodactyl was a good coloured red with very long, clean head, the best of legs and feet, and the straight stern so much desired by German breeders. He was a clean outcross on the dam's side and was, therefore, very valuable as a stud dog, as inbreeding had begun to tell its tale at this date. Another Dachshund whose name appears in most of the pedigrees of the present day winners is Jingle (24,845), a grand red dog with a very long head, beautiful outline of body, and a straight tapering stern. He was kicked by a horse and injured in the shoulder when a puppy, which prevented his ever being shown. His breeding, by Charkow (sire of Jackdaw) ex Joan of Arc, was of the best. Some of the best Dachshunds by Jingle were Janet (27,091), John o' Groat (29,182), Minimus II. (29,184), Duckmanton Winkle (29,178), and Chimes (29,194), all of them big winners and especially good in head. In 1890 Jack Twopence (29,181) and Reena (29,212) won their first prizes, and continued to win for many years for Captain and Mrs. Barry.

The first Dachshunds to be shown, combining the Jackdaw and Pterodactyl blood, were Junket (34,080), Wodin (36,494) a (very successful sire), Washington (36,493), Primula (36,525), Wiseacre (38,713), and Belle Blonde (38,728). The

131

three last-named had a most successful career on the show bench. Janita (36,511), a beautiful red by Maximus, bred by Mr. Walker, came out and took all before her at Portsmouth, beating Pterodactyl for the specials. She had a deep chest, good loin and straight stern. Mr. P. Bradley bred a very nice, small red dog that did a lot of winning, namely, King Sol (38,716), by Minimus II. (29,184) ex Mayflower by Maximus. Mr. Bradley bred another good dog in 1894, this being Erl King (40,726), by Minimus II. ex Mayflower,

TIGER (never exhibited).
Sire TIGER REINECKE. *Dam* ACHMARIENE II.

which much resembled King Sol in type. Kilmanock Cornstalk (40,732), a very good, red dog with an exceptional head, was bred by Mr. W. M. Smyth and won many prizes. Another dog that took a lot of beating was Mrs. Hall's Daphnephoria (38,737), by Jack Twopence, a very good black and tan, having a long head and ears of nice length, well set on.

132

Ch. Wirral Hollybranch.

In 1894 separate classes were given for dapples. The writer purchased Schnippchen (36,529) at the Spa Show in 1893. She was the dam of the dapple dog securing first and special at Berlin in 1892. He also imported from Herr Benda, Achmarienie II. (38,727), which had won prizes at Berlin; and Mr. G. R. Krehl imported Unser Fritz (38,722). In 1895 the writer purchased Tiger Reinecke (462A), one of the best known dapples on the show bench and, in Germany, at trials underground. From these dogs have been bred most of the dapple Dachshunds now in this country. They have at different times been crossed with the black and tan and red dogs.

Wiseacre did a great deal of winning for Mr. Woodiwiss. He was a small dog, very low to the ground, had good bone, and was quite sound. He was by Pterodactyl ex a Jackdaw-bred bitch and was a great success at the stud. One of his best sons was Walwin 96.(586B). Doreen (801A), shown by Mrs. Blackwell, was one of the many good Dachshunds bred by Wodin (36,494) ex Drachenfel (36,503). Doreen was the foundation of a very strong kennel for Mrs. Blackwell. Mrs. Blackwell later on imported the red dog Rother Beelzebub (1,119F). This dog was not only a success on the show bench but was a very successful sire. He was quite the type required for an outcross, and possessed three good properties sadly wanting in many of the prize winners of to-day—courage, powerful jaw, and a straight stern.

In 1897 Captain and Mrs. Barry exhibited Bock Bier (93-554B). This dog was a complete outcross, and it is a great pity that breeders did not make more use of him at stud; he had many desirable points which the in-bred Dachshunds of the day lack. Mr. Percy Haywood exhibited Hotspur (567B) with great success. He was a very taking little dog, combining strength and quality. He was by Pterodactyl out of a Jackdaw-bred bitch and has proved a valuable sire. Some judges took exception to his hind action which accounted for his various placings in the lists of awards.

In 1898 three good dogs were brought out and have proved themselves valuable sires, namely, Brandesburton Magister (473C), Brandesburton Maximus (178C), and Suakes Prince (154C). To one or other of these many of the winners at the present time trace back. A still more successful sire was bred in 1898, namely, Sloan (500C), a dog which has done so much to bring Mr. Lever's kennel to the strong position it now occupies. Carmen Sylva (434E) has quite made Mr. A. Bradbury's kennel by breeding such dogs as Hollyberry (1,108F) and Wirral Hollybranch (219H).

The prize winning Dachshund of to-day is often too large. Breeders at the present time appear to lose sight of the fact that the Dachshund is, in his own country, a sporting dog, bred for work, and capable of going to ground. When the Dachshund Club fixed the limit of 21 lbs. for dogs and 18 lbs. for bitches, the weights were fixed—twenty-five years ago—from the most typical dogs of that time. Xaverl only weighed 18½ lbs., and a large number of the winning dogs did not weigh more than 16 to 17 lbs. It has been proposed to raise the weights fixed in 1881 to suit the show dog of to-day. It will be a great pity if the proposal is adopted. Thusnelda (see page 464) was only 15 lbs., Joan of Arc (see page 466) 15½ lbs., Joubert (see page 466) 16 lbs., Wagtail (see page 467) 15 lbs., and Jackdaw (see page 467) never over 18 lbs. The present day dogs are suffering from in-breeding and, by selection, they are getting much too large. When seen at a show they appear a tired lot, and have certainly not the courage and activity of their ancestors.

To really know and fully appreciate the Dachshund one must see him at his own game, finding and marking foxes and badgers underground. He is a light-hearted, merry companion ; and the writer has always noticed that the hardy Dachshund, and one that has been properly entered and is good at his work, is far more sensible, a better companion and better tempered than the shy, delicate animal so often seen at our shows.

In 1895, after having visited several of the important shows held on the Continent, the writer was more impressed than ever that the type being bred for in this country was wrong, and that the weakness, shyness, and general unsoundness were to a large extent due to in-breeding. He, therefore, in this year imported four Dachshunds from

MRS. DEWAR'S CH. LENCHEN.

Germany, all big winners, both at shows and at trials. They were all sound dogs with strong jaws and straight sterns, and none of them exceeded 17 lbs. weight. The English breeders, however, did not make use of the dogs, so that they did little or no good to the breed in this country. Now, great difficulty is experienced in importing dogs owing to the strict quarantine regulations.

The Teckel-Klub has done a great deal to preserve the type in Germany by holding trials at the important shows;

its stud book, full of information of all kinds concerning the Dachshund, is most interesting. The Teckel-Klub has always acknowledged three varieties of the breed—the short haired, the rough haired, and the long haired. The last-named are not very numerous, and appear to be bred by a very few exhibitors, though classes are given for them at the important shows. The rough haired variety is much more numerous and dogs of this class often compete successfully at the trials.

The following is the description of the breed as adopted by the Dachshund Club :—

DESCRIPTION.

Head and Skull Long, level, and narrow ; peak well developed ; no stop ; eyes intelligent, and somewhat small ; follow body in colour. *Ears*—Long, broad, and soft ; set on low and well back ; carried close to the head. *Jaw*— Strong, level and square to the muzzle ; canines recurvent. *Chest*—Deep and narrow ; breast bone prominent. *Legs and Feet*—Fore legs very short and strong in bone, well crooked, not standing over ; elbows well clothed with muscle, neither in nor out ; feet large, round, and strong, with thick pads and strong nails. Hind legs smaller in bone and higher, hind feet smaller. The dog must stand true, *i.e.*, equally on all parts of the foot. *Skin and Coat*—Skin thick, loose, supple, and in great quantity ; coat dense, short and strong. *Loin*—Well arched, long and muscular. *Stern*—Long and strong, flat at root, tapering to the tip ; hair on under side coarse ; carried low except when excited. Quarters very muscular. *Body*—Length from back of head to root of stern, two and a half times the height at shoulder. Fore ribs well sprung, back ribs very short. *Colour*—Any colour, nose to follow body colour ; much white objectionable. *Symmetry and Quality*—The Dachshund should be long, low and graceful, not cloddy. *Weight*—Dogs about 21lbs., bitches about 18lbs.

HARRY JONES.

We are indebted to Mr. William Loeffler for the following comprehensive, entertaining special article on the little understood Dachshund:

Of the many breeds of dogs in existence, none have gained more friends and won more hearts and a stronger hold in American home in a comparative short time than the Dachshund.

Those who have not seen a single specimen and are entirely ignorant regarding his characteristics, know him by continued caricature.

For centuries back he was the most favored pet of German aristocracy, carefully guarded and upheld in his purity, and it was only occasionally that an outsider received a specimen. A gift of a Dachshund was considered a token of high esteem.

Though he has not lost a particle of his prestige in this respect, and has strong admirers

True Dachshund Specimens.

in the royal families of Europe, he is rapidly becoming a cosmopolitan; with his little crooked legs he now travels over many lands, making friends wherever he lands.

At all times Dachshunde were in charge of professional hunters, who developed their instinct for hunting wonderfully, and the courage, endurance and strength exhibited in pursuing their game is astonishing and marvelous.

The long body, short and muscular legs, the entire strength being centered in his deep chest, indicate that he is intended for work under ground.

To attack a badger or a fox in his own burrow requires bravery of a high degree, especially as the dog is in most cases much smaller than his game. He relies upon the strength of his jaws and his wonderfully developed set of teeth for his work and does not snap or bite at random, but his attack is usually well aimed and effective.

The game-keeper's duty is to destroy all enemies of the game intrusted to his care, consequently foxes, badgers, minks and other vermin are at all times subject to extermination, and the Dachshund is his untiring and able assistant in this work.

His scenting power is of the keenest and he will locate his prey very quickly when he strikes a trail. A fox generally leaves his burrow when the dog enters his domain and falls a victim to the gunner's aim; not so with the badger, who crawl into a corner of his burrow, and two dogs in most cases attack him from different entries, and finally crowd him so that he will stay at bay. The location of the badger can easily be given by the barking of the dogs, and the hunter digs down with pick and spade, when the ground permits such work, until the badger can be seen. By means of a fork pushed over his neck the badger is held and captured.

The Dachshund is also invaluable for finding wounded deer; for which purpose the hunter usually chains the dog, who then leads his master over the trail to locate the game.

At home the Dachshund's disposition changes entirely; he is now a most affectionate and docile animal, and shows by his every expression his attachment for his master and his family. His intelligence is surprising; as a watch or house dog he has few equals, the slightest disturbance will not escape his keen senses and the alarm is given. Most always one member of the family he selects as his special idol, in many cases a child, and it is amusing to watch him, how he does everything in his power to show his affection, following every step taken by his beloved friend. He will frolic for hours and never seem to tire or lose his good temper, and he is always on hand when wanted. He knows the friends of the family and never molests them, but he will not tolerate tramps.

The color of the Dachshund is of great variety, the original stock being black and tan, from which later developed chocolate and tan, gray and tan and single color red, ranging from fawn to dark mahogany red. The spotted Dachshund, such as black and tan as a ground color showing silver gray patches of irregular sizes throughout the black field is of comparatively recent development. Most all have short and glossy coats.

The unusual shape of this dog, combined with a beautiful color, the graceful and dignified walk, the aristocratic bearing, will draw the attention and admiration of every one who sees him.

THE DACHSHUND

PERSONS unfamiliar with the sporting properties of this long-bodied breed are apt to refer smilingly to the Dachshund as " the dog that is sold by the yard," and few even of those who know him give credit to the debonair little fellow for the grim work which he is intended to perform in doing battle with the vicious badger in its lair. Dachshund means " badger dog," and it is a title fairly and squarely earned in his native Germany.

Given proper training, he will perform the duties of several sporting breeds rolled into one. Possessing a wonderful nose, combined with remarkable steadiness, his kind will work out the coldest scent, and once fairly on the line they will give plenty of music and get over the ground at a pace almost incredible. Dachshunds hunt well in a pack, and, though it is not their recognised vocation, they can be successfully used on hare, on fox, and any form of vermin that wears a furry coat. But his legitimate work is directed against the badger, in locating the brock under ground, worrying and driving him into his innermost earth, and there holding him until dug out. It is no part of his calling to come to close grips, though that often happens in the confined space in which he has to work. In this position a badger with his powerful claws digs with such energy and skill as rapidly to bury himself, and the Dachshund needs to be provided with such apparatus as will permit him to clear his way and keep in touch with his formidable quarry. The badger is also hunted by Dachshunds above ground, usually in the mountainous parts of Germany, and in the growing crops of maize, on the lower slopes, where the vermin work terrible havoc in the evening. In this case the badger is rounded up and driven by the dogs up to the guns which are posted between the game and their earths. For this sport the dog used is heavier, coarser, and of larger build, higher on the leg, and more generally houndy in appearance. Dachshunds are frequently used for deer driving, in which operation they are especially valuable, as they work slowly, and do not frighten or‐ overrun their quarry, and can penetrate the densest undergrowth. Packs of Dachshunds may sometimes be engaged on wild boar, and, as they are web-footed and excellent swimmers, there is no doubt that their terrier qualities would make them useful assistants to the Otterhound. Apropos of their capabilities in the water it is the case that a year or two ago, at Offenbach-on-Main, at some trials arranged for life-saving by dogs, a Dachshund carried off the first prize against all comers.

As a companion in the house the Dachshund has perhaps no compeer. He is a perfect gentleman ; cleanly in his habits, obedient, unobtrusive, incapable of smallness, affectionate, very sensitive to rebuke or to unkindness, and amusingly jealous. As a watch he is excellent, quick to detect a strange footstep, valiant to defend the threshold, and to challenge with deep voice any intruder, yet sensibly discerning his master's friends, and not annoying them with prolonged growling and grumbling as many terriers do when a stranger is admitted. Properly brought up, he is a perfectly safe and amusing companion for children, full of animal spirits, and ever ready to share in a romp, even though it be accompanied by rough and tumble play. In Germany, where he is the most popular of all dogs, large or small, he is to be found in every home, from the Emperor's palace downwards, and his quaint appearance, coupled with his entertaining personality, is daily seized upon by the comic papers to illustrate countless jokes at his expense.

The origin of the Dachshund is not very clear. Some

writers have professed to trace the breed or representations of it on the monuments of the Egyptians. Some aver that it is a direct descendant of the French Basset-hound, and others that he is related to the old Turnspits—the dogs so excellent in kitchen service, of whom Dr. Caius wrote that " when any meat is to be roasted they go into a wheel, where they, turning about with the weight of their bodies, so diligently look to their business that no drudge nor scullion can do the feat more cunningly, whom the popular sort hereupon term Turnspits." Certainly the dog commonly used in this occupation was long of body and short of leg, very much resembling the Dachshund.

In all probability the Dachshund is a manufactured breed—a breed evolved from a large type of hound intermixed with a terrier to suit the special conditions involved in the pursuit and extermination of a quarry that, unchecked, was capable of seriously interfering with the cultivation of the land. He comprises in his small person the characteristics of both hound and terrier—his wonderful powers of scent, his long, pendulous ears, and, for his size, enormous bone, speak of his descent from the hound that hunts by scent. In many respects he favours the Bloodhound, and one may often see Dachshunds which, having been bred from parents carefully selected to accentuate some fancy point, have exhibited the very pronounced " peak " (occipital bone), the protruding haw of the eye, the loose dewlap and the colour markings characteristic of the Bloodhound. His small stature, iron heart, and willingness to enter the earth bespeak the terrier cross.

The Dachshund was first introduced to this country in sufficient numbers to merit notice in the early 'sixties, and, speedily attracting notice by his quaint formation and undoubted sporting instincts, soon became a favourite. At first appearing at shows in the " Foreign Dog " class, he quickly received a recognition of his claims to more favoured treatment, and was promoted by the Kennel Club to a special classification as a sporting dog. Since then his rise has been rapid, and he now is reckoned as one of the numerically largest breeds exhibited. Unfortunately, however, he has been little, if ever, used for sport in the sense that applies in Germany, and this fact, coupled with years of breeding from too small a stock (or stock too nearly related) and the insane striving after the fanciful and exaggerated points demanded by judges at dog shows, many of whom never saw a Dachshund at his legitimate work, has seriously affected his usefulness. He has deteriorated in type, lost grit and sense, too, and is often a parody of the true type of Dachshund that is to be found in his native land.

To the reader who contemplates possessing one or more Dachshunds a word of advice may be offered. Whether you want a dog for sport, for show, or as a companion, endeavour to get a good one—a well-bred one. To arrive at this do not buy from an advertisement on your own knowledge of the breed, but seek out an expert amateur breeder and exhibitor, and get his advice and assistance. If you intend to start a kennel for show purposes, do not buy a high-priced dog at a show, but start with a well-bred bitch, and breed your own puppies, under the guidance of the aforementioned expert. In this way, and by rearing and keeping your puppies till they are of an age to be exhibited, and at the same time carefully noting the awards at the best shows, you will speedily learn which to retain and the right type of dog to keep and breed for, and in future operations you will be able to discard inferior puppies at an earlier age. But it is a great mistake, if you intend to form a kennel for show purposes, to sell or part with your puppies too early. It is notorious with all breeds that puppies change very much as they grow. The best looking in the nest often go wrong later, and the ugly duckling turns out the best of the litter. This is especially true of Dachshunds, and it requires an expert to pick the best puppy of a litter at a month or two old, and even he may be at fault unless the puppy is exceptionally well reared.

To rear Dachshund puppies successfully you must not overload them with fat—give them strengthening food that does not lay on flesh. Lean, raw beef, finely chopped, is an excellent food once or twice a day for the first few months, and, though this comes expensive, it pays in the end. Raw meat is supposed to cause worm troubles, but these pests are also found where meat is not given, and in any case a puppy is fortified with more strength to withstand them if fed on raw meat than otherwise, and a good dosing from time to time will be all that is necessary to keep him well and happy.

Young growing puppies must have their freedom to gambol about, and get their legs strong. Never keep the puppies cooped up in a small kennel run or house. If you have a fair-sized yard, give them the run of that, or even the garden, in spite of what your gardener may say—they may do a little damage to the flowers, but will assuredly do good to themselves. They love to dig in the soft ·borders : digging is second nature to them, and is of great importance in their development.

If you have not a garden, or if the flowers are too sacred, it is better to place your puppies as early as possible with respectable cottagers, or small farmers, especially the latter, with whom they will have entire freedom to run about, and will not be overfed.

If you intend to show your puppies, you should begin some time in advance to school them to walk on the lead and to stand quiet when ordered to. Much depends on this in the judging ring, where a dog who is unused to being on a lead often spoils his chances of appearing at his best under the (to him) strange experiences of restraint which the lead entails.

During the past five-and-twenty years the names of two particular Dachshunds stand out head and shoulders above those of their competitors : Champions Jackdaw and Pterodactyl. Jackdaw had a wonderful record, having, during a long show career, never been beaten in his class from start to finish, and having won many valuable prizes. He was credited with being the most perfect Dachshund that had ever been seen in England, and probably as good as anything in Germany.

Ch. Jackdaw was a black and tan dog, bred and owned by Mr. Harry Jones, of Ipswich. He was sired by Ch. Charkow, out of Wagtail, and born 20th July, 1886. Through his dam he was descended from a famous bitch, Thusnelda, who was imported by Mr. Mudie in the early 'eighties. She was a winner of high honours in Hanover. The name of Jackdaw figures in all the best pedigrees of to-day.

Ch. Pterodactyl was born in 1888, and bred by Mr. Willink. He was in a measure an outcross from the standard type of the day, and his dam, whose pedigree is in dispute, was thought to have been imported. After passing through one or two hands he was purchased by Mr. Harry Jones, and in his kennel speedily made a great name in the show ring and at the stud, and was eventually sold for a high price to Mr. Sidney Woodiwiss, who at that period had the largest kennel of Dachshunds in England.

" Ptero," as he was called, was a big, light red dog, with wonderful fore-quarters and great muscular development. He also possessed what is called a " punishing jaw " and rather short ears, and looked a thorough " business " dog. He had an almost unbroken series of successes at shows in England, and. being taken to Germany (in the days before the quarantine regulations), he took the highest honours in the heavy-weight class, and a special prize for the best Dachshund of all classes. This dog became the favourite sire of his day and the fashionable colour.

The black and tan thereupon went quite out of favour, and this fact, coupled with the reckless amount of inbreeding of red to red that has been going on since Ptero's day, accounts largely for the prevalence of light eyes, pink noses, and bad-coloured coats of the Dachshunds, as a class, to-day.

There are, strictly speaking, three varieties of Dachshund—(a) the short-haired, (b) the long-haired, and (c) the rough-haired.

Of these we most usually find the first-named in England, and they are no doubt the original stock. Of the others, though fairly numerous in Germany, very few are to be seen in this country, and although one or two have been imported the type has never seemed to appeal to exhibitors.

Both the long-haired and rough-haired varieties have no doubt been produced by crosses with other breeds, such as the Spaniel and probably the Irish Terrier, respectively.

In the long-haired variety the hair should be soft and wavy, forming lengthy plumes under the throat, lower parts of the body, and the backs of the legs, and it is longest on the under side of the tail, where it forms a regular flag like that of a Setter or Spaniel. The rough-haired variety shows strongly a terrier cross by his " varmint " expression and short ears.

The Germans also subdivide by colour, and again for show purposes by weight. These subdivisions are dealt with in their proper order in the standard of points, and it is only necessary to say here that all the varieties, colours, and weights are judged by the same standard except in so far as they differ in texture of coat. At the same time the Germans themselves do not regard the dapple Dachshunds as yet so fixed in type as the original coloured dogs, and this exception must also apply to the long and the rough haired varieties.

The following German standard of points embodies a detailed description of the breed :—

General Appearance and Disposition—In general appearance the Dachshund is a very long and low dog, with compact and well-muscled body, resting on short, slightly crooked fore-legs. A long head and ears, with bold and defiant carriage and intelligent expression. In disposition the Dachshund is full of spirit, defiant when attacked, aggressive even to foolhardiness when attacking; in play amusing and untiring; by nature wilful and unheeding. Head—Long, and appearing conical from above, and from a side view, tapering to the point of the muzzle, wedge-shaped. The skull should be broad rather than narrow, to allow plenty of brain room, sightly arched, and fairly straight, without a stop, but not deep or snipy. Eyes—Medium in size, oval, and set obliquely, with very clear, sharp expression and of a dark colour, except in the case of the liver and tan, when the eyes may be yellow ; and in the dapple, when the eyes may be light or " wall-eyed." Nose—Preferably deep black. The flesh-coloured and spotted

149

noses are allowable only in the liver and tan and dapple varieties. **Ears**—Set on moderately high, or, seen in profile, above the level of the eyes, well back, flat, not folded, pointed, or narrow, hanging close to the cheeks, very mobile, and when at attention carried with the back of the ear upward and outward. **Neck**—Moderately long, with slightly arched nape, muscular and clean, showing no dewlap, and carried well up and forward. **Fore-quarters**—His work underground demands strength and compactness, and, therefore, the chest and shoulder regions should be deep, long, and wide. The shoulder blade should be long, and set on very sloping, the upper arm of equal length with, and at right angles to, the shoulder blade, strong-boned and well-muscled, and lying close to ribs, but moving freely. The lower arm is slightly bent inwards, and the feet should be turned slightly outwards, giving an appearance of " crooked " legs approximating to the cabriole of a Chippendale chair. Straight, narrow, short shoulders are always accompanied by straight, short, upper arms, forming an obtuse angle, badly developed brisket and " keel " or chicken breast, and the upper arm being thrown forward by the weight of the body behind causes the legs to knuckle over at the " knees." Broad, sloping shoulders, on the other hand, insure soundness of the fore-legs and feet. **Legs and Feet**—Fore-legs very short and strong in bone, slightly bent inwards ; seen in profile, moderately straight and never bending forward or knuckling over. Feet large, round, and strong, with thick pads, compact and well-arched toes, nails strong and black. The dog must stand equally on all parts of the foot. **Body**—Should be long and muscular, the chest very oval, rather than very narrow and deep, to allow ample room for heart and lungs, hanging low between front legs, the brisket point should be high and very prominent, the ribs well sprung out towards the loins (not flat-sided). Loins short and strong. The line of back only slightly depressed behind shoulders and only slightly arched over loins. The hind-quarters should not be higher than the shoulders, thus giving a general appearance of levelness. **Hind-quarters**—The rump round, broad, and powerfully muscled ; hip bone not too short, but broad and sloping ; the upper arm, or thigh, thick, of good length, and jointed at right angles to the hip bone. The lower leg (or second thigh) is, compared with other animals, short, and is set on at right angles to the upper thigh, and is very firmly muscled. The hind-legs are lighter in bone than the front ones, but very strongly muscled, with well-rounded-out buttocks, and the knee joint well developed. Seen from behind, the legs should be wide apart and straight, and not cowhocked. The dog should not be higher at the quarters than at shoulder. **Stern**—Set on fairly high, strong at root, and tapering, but not too long. Neither too much curved nor carried too high ; well, but not too much, feathered ; a bushy tail is better than too little hair. **Coat and Skin**—Hair short and close as possible, glossy and smooth, but resistant to the touch if stroked the wrong way. The skin tough and elastic, but fitting close to the body. **Colour**—*One Coloured :*— There are several self-colours recognised, including deep red, yellowish red, smutty red. Of these the dark, or cherry, red is preferable, and in this colour light shadings on any part of the body or head are undesirable. " Black " is rare, and is only a sport from black and tan. *Two*

Coloured :—Deep black, brown (liver) or grey, with golden or tan markings (spots) over the eyes at the side of the jaw and lips, inner rim of ears, the breast, inside and back of legs, the feet, and under the tail for about one-third of its length. In the above-mentioned colours white markings are objectionable. The utmost that is allowed being a small spot, or a few hairs, on the chest. *Dappled :*—A silver grey to almost white foundation colour, with dark, irregular spots (small for preference) of dark grey, brown, tan, or black. The general appearance should be a bright, indefinite coloration, which is considered especially useful in a hunting dog. **Weight**—Dachshunds in Germany are classified by weight as follows :—*Light-weight*—Dogs up to 16½ lb., bitches up to 15½ lb. *Middle-weight*—Dogs up to 22 lb., bitches up to 22 lb. *Heavy-weight*—Over 22 lb. *Toys*—Up to 12 lb. The German pound is one-tenth more than the English. The light-weight dog is most used for going to ground.

This is a German variety of dog, and one that has undergone considerable change through selection. Like the Basset-hound it exists in rough and smooth-coated varieties, though the latter is the one that finds most favour. The chief use of the Dachshund in Great Britain is for companionship only, for which purposes the breed is highly esteemed, more especially by the ladies. In Germany the Dachshund is used for hunting, but it has a much more workmanlike appearance than the British type of hound. In height the Dachshund should measure from 7 to 9 inches, such measurement being taken from the shoulder, whilst the weight ranges from 18 to 21 lbs. In Germany the clubs have three divisions of weight, namely, light, medium and heavy; the medium weight being the most preferable one. The coat should be short and close, whilst the skin ought to be loose and abundant all over the body.

With reference to colour, Dachshunds exist either in whole or parti-colours, but red, yellow and fawn are the principal ones, whilst black-and-tan, chocolate and-tan, also dapple, are the parti-colours usually met with. Pure white Dachshunds are exceedingly rare. The presence of much white hair on the body is regarded with disfavour. The nostrils must correspond to the body colour; for instance, a chocolate-and-tan dog must have a liver-coloured nose, and a black-and-tan dog a black nose.

The conformation of the Dachshund is peculiar in many respects, the length of the limbs being altogether disproportionate to that of the body. It is a variety of dog which preserves an element of hound characteristics in the region of the head, but the reduction in the length of the limbs abolishes one of the leading characteristics of hounds, viz., speed. The body should be long, two and a half times the height at the shoulder—in fact length of body and crook of the fore limbs constitute points of the greatest importance. The loins must be well arched, the chest deep, and the back ribs well-sprung. Amplitude of chest capacity is indispensable, so that the chest must be deep, but a narrow chest and prominent breast bones are requisite qualifications.

The head must be long and narrow, and the dome

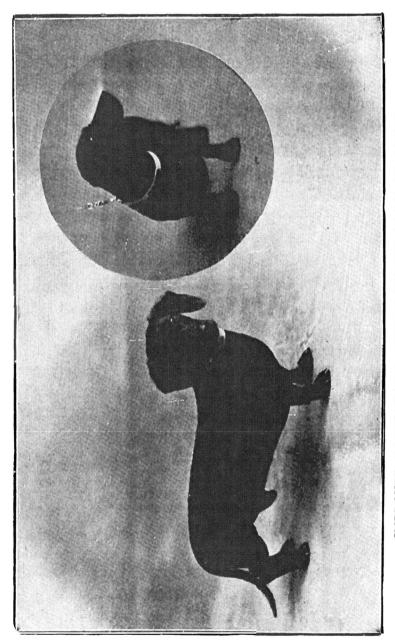

IMPROVED DACHSHUNDS. THE PROPERTY OF MR. W. LEVER

To face page 192

of the skull well developed. The ears long, broad and soft; thin in the leather, and carried close to the side of the head. Muzzle long, rather square in outline, with the lower jaw bearing sound, level teeth. There must be no evidence of "stop." In looking at the Dachshund it will be noticed that the shoulders are prominent, being big boned and heavily muscled in this region. The eyes to be of medium size, and the same colour as the body. Particular attention is paid to the fore limbs, which must be short, with elbows lying close to the ribs. The shortness of the forearm and the relatively large size of the bone in this region, together with the crook at the knees and short pasterns and broad feet, are significant characteristics of the Dachshund. The English and the German Dachshund clubs differ in their code of points, therefore it would be as well to enumerate the German standard of points, the description of which is as follows:

Colour.—(*a*) Single-coloured: red, yellowish-red, yellow, or red-and-yellow with black points, but one colour only is preferable, and red is better than yellowish-red and yellow. White is also allowed. Nose and nails black, red also permitted, but not desirable

(*b*) Two-coloured: deep black or brown, or grey, each with yellow or reddish-brown spots over the eyes, on the sides of the jaws and lower lips, on the

156

inner rim of ear, on the breast, on the inside and back of legs, under the tail, and from there down one-third to one-half of the under-side of the tail. Nose and nails black in black dogs, brown in brown dogs, grey in grey dogs, and also flesh-colour.

In one- and two-coloured dogs white is permissible, but only to the smallest possible extent, as spot or small streaks on breast.

(c) Spotted: ground is a shining silver-grey, or even white, with dark, irregular spots (large spots are undesirable) of dark grey, brown, yellowish-red or black.

Neither the light nor the dark colours should predominate. The main factor is such a general appearance that at some distance the dog shall show an indefinite and varied colour which renders him particularly useful as a hunting dog. The russet-brown marks are darker in darker spotted dogs, and yellower in the lighter ones, and there may be an indication of these in the case of a white foundation. Light eyes are permitted; when the ground colour is white a flesh-coloured or spotted nose is not a fault. White marks are not desirable in dark dogs, but are not to be regarded as faults which disqualify.

Height at Shoulder.—7¼ to 8⅜ inches.

Coat.—Short, thick as possible, glossy, greasy (not harsh and dry), equally covering entire body (never showing bare spots).

Weight.—This is divided into three classes, viz., light weight: dogs under 16½ lbs., bitches under 15½ lbs. Medium weight: dogs from 16½ lbs. to 22 lbs., bitches 15½ to 22 lbs. Heavy weight: dogs and bitches over 22 lbs.

Head.—Elongated, and, as seen from above and from the side, tapering towards the point of the nose, sharply outlined and finely modelled, particularly in profile.

Skull.—Neither too wide nor too narrow, only slightly arched, and running gradually without break (stop)—the less the break (stop) the better the type—into a well-defined and slightly-arched nasal bone

Eyes.—Medium-sized, oval, set obliquely, clear and energetical expression. Except the silver colour of the grey and spotted dogs, and the yellow eyes of the brown dogs, the colour is a transparent brown.

Nose.—Point and root long and slender, very finely formed.

Lips.—Tightly stretched, well covering the lower jaw, neither deep nor snipy, with corner of mouth slightly marked.

Jaws.—Capable of opening wide, extending to behind the eyes.

Teeth.—Well-developed, particularly the corner teeth, these latter fitting exactly. Incisors fitting each other or the inner side of the upper incisors touching the outer side of the lower.

Ears.—Relatively well back, high and well set on, with forward edge lying close to the cheeks; very broad and long, beautifully rounded (not narrow, pointed or folded), very movable, as in all intelligent dogs; when at attention the back of the ear directed forwards and upwards.

Neck.—Sufficiently long, muscular, lean, no dewlap, slightly arched in the nape, running in graceful lines between the shoulders, usually carried high and forward.

Shoulders.—Long, broad and set sloping, lying firmly on fully-developed thorax; muscles hard and plastic.

Chest.—Corresponding with his work underground, muscular, compact; the region of the chest and shoulders deep, long and wide; breast bone strong and so prominent as to show a hollow on each side.

Back.—In the case of sloping shoulders and hind quarters, short and firm; if steep (straight) shoulders and hind quarters, long and weak; line of back behind shoulders only slightly sunk, and only slightly arched near the loins.

Trunk.—Ribs full, oval, with ample width for heart and lungs; deep and hanging low between the fore legs; well sprung out towards the loins; loins short and broad; line of belly moderately drawn up and joined to the hind quarters with loosely-stretched skin.

Hind Quarters.—These must be round, full and broad, muscles hard and plastic; pelvis bone not too short, broad and strongly-developed, set moderately sloping.

Fore Legs.—Upper arm of equal length with and at right angles to the shoulders. Strong-boned, well-muscled and lying close to the ribs, but moving freely up to the shoulder-blade. Lower arms short as compared with other animals, slightly inclined inwards. Strongly muscled and plastic towards front and outside; inside and back parts stretched by hard tendons.

Hind Legs.—Thigh bones strong, of good length, and joined to pelvis at right angles; thighs strong and with hard muscles; buttocks also well rounded out; knee-joint developed in length; lower legs short in comparison with other animals, at right angles to thigh bone, and firmly muscled; ankle bones well apart, with strong, well-sprung heel and broad Achilles tendon.

Feet.—Fore feet broad and sloping outwards; hind feet smaller and narrower; toes always close together, with distinct bend in each toe; nails strong and regularly pointed outwards; thick soles.

Tail.—Set on at medium height, not too long, nor carried too high.

General Appearance.—Gnome-like, short-legged, elongated, but stiff figure, muscular. Notwithstanding the short limbs and long body, neither appearance stunted, awkward, incapable of movement nor yet lean or weasel-like, with a pert, saucy pose of the head, and intelligent expression.

Defects.—Too weak or crippled, too high or too low on the legs; skull too wide, too narrow or too much arched; ears set on too high, too heavy or too short; also set on too low and narrow, or low or slack; "stop" too pronounced, and goggle eyes; nasal bone too short or pressed in; lips too pointed or too deep; overshot; short developed neck; fore legs badly developed, twisted or poorly muscled, hare-footed or flat-spread toes; too deeply sunk behind the shoulders, *i.e.*, hollow-backed; loins too much arched or weak; ribs too flat or too short; rump higher than the shoulders; chest too short or too flat; loins arched like a Greyhound; hind quarters too narrow or poor in muscle; cow-hocked; tail set on high, and carried too high, or too much curled; too thin, long, or hairless (rat-tailed); coat too thick, too coarse, too fine or too thin; colour dead, dull, or too much mixed. In black dogs with russet-brown marks (tan) these latter should not extend too far, particularly on the ears.

The foregoing description of the Dachshund as described by the Germans embodies all the principal features of the English standard, but discloses the fact that continental capacity for taking pains is greater there than in Great Britain.

Kennel Management and Hygiene.—Anyone contemplating the formation of a kennel of Dachshunds should endeavour to select as the foundation-stone for such kennel a fashionable brood bitch or two, and mate these with suitable sires. The constitution of the Dachshund is not particularly hardy, more especially in strains which have been a good deal inbred, nevertheless these hounds cannot be considered as specially difficult to rear, provided that due attention is paid to kennel management in general. The best time of year to breed from bitches is the spring, so that the offspring will have the advantages of the summer weather for exercises and to attain a fair degree of development before the ensuing winter, in this manner fortifying the constitution against the ravages of such diseases as distemper, etc. Dachshunds over twelve months old should be fed night and morning, and a frequent change of food is most beneficial. Half a pound of flesh for each hound, mixed up with a quarter of a pound of soaked stale bread, or the same quantity of Spratt's hound meal, will be found suitable for the evening meal, whilst in the morning biscuits soaked in gravy, or Spratt's oval biscuits given dry, will make an economical and efficient food. Young hounds should be fed three times a day, and food given both dry and soaked. The hound glove must be used regularly as lustre of coat constitutes a matter of considerable importance, especially in the show ring. If necessary to wash, do so on the week previous to the show, so as to give time for the lustre to reassert itself on the coat, which, of course, has been removed by washing. Overfeeding must be avoided, as the Dachshund when too fat loses that looseness of coat so needful in a typical specimen. Exercise must be moderate, that given at a walking pace being the best, as these hounds are precluded from fast work.

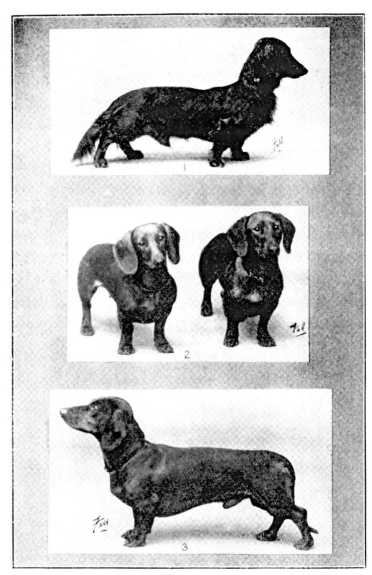

(1). LONG-HAIRED DACHSHUND KATZMANN VON HALSCHTSHOP, the property of Mrs. Quicke, of Tattenham Kennels, Trosley, West Malling, Kent.

(2) and (3). CHATTERIS BELINDA and CHATTERIS SIMON, two red Dachshunds, are the offspring of the prisoner of war 'Bousies,' a red Dachshund captured by the 18th Division in the village of that name east of Le Cateau during the German retreat in October, 1918. 'Bousies' was brought home to England after the armistice by Lt.-Col. B. J. Walker, of 10 Chester Terrace, Regent's Park, London, N.W.1.

In the olden days a dog known as the 'Turnspit,' used by cooks to turn the roasting joints, was a very important member of the domestic staff. From the illustrations and descriptions of the variety it is just possible that the Dachshund is a distant relative.

THE DACHSHUND

A dog with an individuality. At one time it had crooked front legs, but to-day the lower portion of front legs is only slightly bent inwards. Crooked legs caused the dog to knuckle over, and were no aid in digging. On the Continent it is used in the forests for badgers and foxes ; in India and Africa for tracking wounded game. Very courageous and fast in spite of short legs, and a very charming house dog.

There are three kinds : the short-haired, the long-haired, the rough-coated.

The colours are red, black and tans, dappled, liver and tan, etc. When quite young, the puppies are like fox cubs. It has been observed that the puppies do not play with one another as most puppies do.

THE DACHSHUND

Possibly the first illustration of a Dachshund or its close relative the Basset hound.
A wood cut from Aldrovandus, 1637. He names it "A French Dog."

The Dachshund is a breed that may have originated in Germany,[2]
The type has greatly altered, even in the last hundred years or so, and the
present-day breed is very unlike the dog as it was in Germany 150 years
ago. It was more or less recently said by a street urchin, and duly reported
in the Press, that such a dog was a Foxhound that had had its legs worn
down by constantly following bicycles. The long body and short legs of
the Dachshund have always made it a butt of the humorist. It yet remains
the comic-dog of Germany, and is used extensively by the artists of humorous
incident. The Dachshund is founded on an old type of hound, and as
far as I can discover from searching through early books was first mentioned
in 1753 and first illustrated as a Dachshund in a German book in 1780, in
which a couple of these dogs are depicted. This illustration is of considerable
interest, for it bears the words in Latin, *Canis Vertagus*, and in German
Dachshunde.[3] The dogs shown are very much more of the hound type than
the breed is now. Their ears are long, such as are the ears of Basset-

[1] See Plate 38, No. 13.
[2] It is difficult to be certain of this for if the Basset and Dachshund are closely
related ; the original Dachshunds may have come from France.
[3] See Plate 2, No. 6.

hounds, a breed to which they bear a marked resemblance.[1] It would not be surprising to find that the Basset-hound and the Dachshund were one and the same thing,[2] the Dachshunde being the name given to the type in Germany because of the service to which it was put. But very great changes were produced in the breed in the years that followed. It lost the hound head and the hound type, and became much more of a Terrier. How the type was altered to the present-day dog is not easy to say. It is possible that during the eighteenth century the Black-and-tan Terrier of Manchester or a similar dog to it was used. In England the breed first arrived, so it is said, as a present to Her Majesty Queen Victoria, from Saxony. They were, according to *Stonehenge*, " a long, low, and very strong hound, with full head and sweeping ears,"[3] standing 14 to 16 inches from the ground. Their short legs and long bodies, and their very attractive appearance, made them popular, and several further importations were made. Becoming fashionable, they were taken up by many important people in the country. The breed was greatly improved by British breeders, particularly by a Mr. Barrett and a Mr. R. McM. Smyth, whilst earlier breeders were the Earl of Onslow, Mr. Schweizer, and Mr. Fisher, the latter being a successful exhibitor, who had obtained his dogs from the kennels of Prince Edward of Saxe-Weimar. A Mr. Lovell had the hound type Dachshund, *Pixie*, whilst a Mr. Hanbury imported *Fritz*,[4] a red dog of very deep colour, which stood too high on the legs for the true Dachshund, and also a bitch by name of *Dina*,[4] which had a good head and ears. But such dogs were something new and great was the sensation caused at Maidstone when these two were exhibited there. They were, so we read, described to be " an astonishing spectacle," and the judge (what a glimpse this gives of early-day judging, indeed !) was so impressed that to *Dina* he gave a special prize ! If we can read successfully between the lines, we can believe that in Germany the original Dachshund were being crossed and improved. For in the coming of the dog *Haufmann* a distinctly better type arrived in England. But very soon there was to come to England an ugly little dog named *Thusnelda*, a small black-and-tan, imported by Mr. Mudie. Ugly as she undoubtedly was, and with many a bad fault, yet never had she an ugly puppy, and, what is more, she did much to improve the breed, bringing in finer quality, then so badly needed. About 1875[5] *Waldire* arrived, a black-and-tan, coarsely built, with a dark head. She had white feet. She also was to play a part, it was fated, in the making of some of the best dogs that have ever been seen. She bred *Chenda* and *Chenda* bred *Bodo*, and *Bodo* was the sire of *Wag*, and this *Wag* bred with the ugly little bitch *Thusnelda* produced *Wagtail*, and *Wagtail* was the mother of *Charkow*, the noted champion, the property of Mr. Barret Hamilton. But *Charkow*, famous as he was, was yet more famed for his son, *Jackdaw*, the black-and-tan champion. Other important dogs followed. There was *Pterodactyl* and later *Brandesburton Filius*, and Ch. *Honeystone* and *Theo v. Neumarkt*, and the two famous dogs of 1895, Ch. *Belle Blonde* and Ch. *Primula*, both owned by Miss Pigott. Indeed, *Primula* beat

---

[1] See Plate 28, Nos. 7 and 8.

[2] Col. Thornton, in 1806, shows a picture of a *Dachshund* and names it *The French Hound*. He purchased the dog and brought it to England. He writes " he may perhaps be superior to German hounds." Note also Androvandus' illustration on page 151.

[3] It would seem from this that in 1859 the type was yet of the hound type.

[4] See Plate 11, No. 11. *Fritz* and *Dina*.

[5] It is of interest that the following year Dr. Fitzinger's work appeared. He gives the illustration of the types seen on Plate 26, No. 1. A straight legged, a crooked legged, and a long-coated Dachshund. It will here be seen that they are no longer of the hound type as depicted by Riedel.

167

Pterodactyl in 1894. *Pterodactyl* was the property of Mr. Sydney Woodiwiss, and never was there a greater friendship between a dog and a man. Once when Mr. Woodiwiss went to America, *Pterodactyl* was beside himself with agitation, and was able only to rest when given an old suit belonging to his master. The old dog slept on that suit, refusing to sleep anywhere else. When Mr. Woodiwiss returned the dog lost all interest in the old suit, in fact he never went near it again ! *Pterodactyl* died in March, 1897, leaving, amongst other noted dogs, Champions *Belle Blonde, Primula* and Ch. *Wiseacre.* In 1898 a Mrs. Allingham showed a novelty in Dachshunds, a long-coated specimen of the breed. Although such dogs were quite common in Germany,[1] in England this dog was considered so novel that it was always in demand by promoters of charity performances, for it was only necessary to advertise that this little dog would be shown to draw the crowd, anxious to behold so strange a thing. We read that it had been presented to Mrs. Allingham by the Countess Thurn. Mrs. Allingham was a great worker for the breed. It was this lady who offered a hand-painted screen as a prize for the best Dachshund, which was won by Her Royal Highness the Princess of Wales, later to be the much-loved Queen Alexandra. About this time Lady Lonsdale had a special type of Dachshund that no one else in England possessed, and these rare little dogs were Dachshunds with hound-marking, very much such as dogs shown in 1780 by the German artist. The Dachshund had now reached the zenith of its popularity. It was a time of high prices. *Jim Crow*, a son of the noted *Jackdaw*, was sold to Mrs. Castairs by Mr. Harry Jones for three figures. Mr. Krehl introduced the dapple-marked Dachshund to this country, but they never became popular. The reds and black-and-tans held their own. The important dog, *Brandesburton Filius*, was the sire of the remarkable dog Ch. *Honeystone*, which did much to make the breed smaller and to produce more character. Then into the breed came the dog *Theo. v. Neumarkt*, which to-day ranks as the most important of all breeding. *Theo. v. Neumarkt*, unfortunately, died whilst still young, unfortunate indeed for the breed, for undoubtedly he was the most powerful improving influence of recent times.

The Dachshund Club was formed in 1881, on January 17, and Mr. Montague Wootten was its first hon. secretary. Many cups were given to the breed. I give the winners of the fifty-guinea Challenge Cup, presented in 1884, and won outright by Major Harry Jones in 1896—a trophy hard fought for and well won ! It is an interesting list, for it shows the position *Jackdaw* held, for it was he that won the cup outright. The winners were *Jackdaw* with eleven wins, *Maximus* four, *Lady* three, *Pterodactyl* three, *Belle Blonde* two, *Joan of Arc* two, *Wiseacre* one, *Belgian Herr* one, *Primute* one.

The present-day winning dogs are for the most part a continuation of the German and British strains, and are descended from *Brandesburton Filius*, Ch. *Mian v. Waldendacht*, *Theo. v. Newmarkt*, Ch. *Faust v. Forstenberg*, and Ch. *Remagen-Max*. *Brandesburton Filius* was a son of *Racker-Weber*. *B. Filius* was imported about 1904. He is described to be a short-backed " cobby " dog, and although by no means a perfect specimen, was able to counteract the big, coarse, clumsy, long-eared Dachshunds which had then become very commonly met with.

It was from one of his stock that Miss Thompson's noted Yorkshire kennel was founded. It is also from *B. Filius* that Major Hayward bred his great dog, Ch. *Honeystone*, who for years was unbeatable. A son of this dog is exhibited on Plate 26, No. 8. Amongst recent bitches, Ch. *Wanda*

[1] They were known in Germany in 1875.

von Luitpoldsheim, owned by Mrs. Bradbury, was one of the most beautiful Dachshunds ever seen. Unfortunately, she died quite young.[1]

In the wiry-coated Dachshunds, the more wiry the coat the better, whilst in the long-coated type the coat is desired to be long and silky, especially on the legs, tail, and ears.[2] The weight of the Dachshund has shown a decrease in the last few years, indeed the lighter dog, with more quality, is the more popular.

Dachshunds mature slowly, and during their growing up change considerably in appearance, and it is only when they finally settle down as dogs of a year or more that the type appears to be fixed. To keep the colour great care must be used. If reds are bred to reds too frequently the noses, which should be black, gradually become flesh-coloured, and the eyes, which should be dark, become light. To prevent this, reds are mated with black-and-tan occasionally. In reds, a red nose *is* permissible, but not desirable. If reds are mated with chocolate-and-tan, light eyes and flesh-coloured noses appear. The black-and-tan are very handsome, and the tan should be of a very rich colour. Pale tan often occurs in very inbred dogs. In chocolate-and-tan the nose is usually flesh-coloured, and the eyes are light. Dapples are allowed to have one or both eyes—*wall eyes*.

In recent years we find Mr. T. A. Lever and Major P. C. G. Hayward, M.B.E., as the owners of the most important exhibition kennels. Before the war Major Hayward's *Honeystone*, already mentioned, carried everything before him. After the war his *Honeystick* was one of the leading champions. Mr. T. A. Lever brought his *Scotch Pearl*, and Mr. J. J. Holgate his *Mohikaner von Birkbusch*. Miss F. E. Dixon[3] showed her great champion *Karkof*, Miss N. McGinnis her *Remagen Max*, and Mrs. N. Bradbury her *Wanda von Luitpoldscheim*. Miss D. Spurrier exhibited her *Silva von Luitpoldsheim*. George Meredith[4] wrote on the Dachshund:—

"Our Islet out of Helgoland dismissed from his quaint tenement, quits hates and loves.
There lived with us a wagging humorist in that hound's arch dwarf-legged on boxing gloves."

169

THE DACHSHUND.

General Appearance : Long and low, but with compact and well-muscled body, neither crippled, cloddy nor clumsy, with bold, defiant carriage of head and intelligent expression. **Head and Skull :** Long, and appearing conical when seen from above, and from a side view tapering to the point of the muzzle. Stop not pronounced and skull should be slightly arched in profile, and appearing neither too broad nor too narrow. **Eyes :** Medium in size, oval, and set obliquely. Dark in colour, except in the case of chocolates, which may be lighter, and in dapples one or both wall eyes are permissible. **Ears :** Broad, of moderate length and well rounded (not narrow, pointed, or folded) relatively well back, high, and well set on, lying close to the cheek, very mobile as in all intelligent dogs, when at attention the back of the ear directed forward and outward. **Jaw :** Neither too square nor snipy, but strong, lips lightly stretched, fairly covering the lower jaw. **Neck :** Sufficiently long, muscular, clean, no dewlap, slightly arched in the nape, running in graceful lines into the shoulders, carried well up and forward. **Forequarters :** Shoulder blades long, broad, and set on sloping, lying firmly on fully-developed ribs or thorax, muscles hard and plastic. **Chest :** Very oval, with ample room for heart and lungs, deep and well sprung-out ribs towards the loins, breast-bone prominent. **Legs and Feet :** Forelegs very short and in proportion to size, strong in bone. Upper arm of equal length with and at right angles to shoulder blade, elbows lying close to ribs but moving freely up to shoulder blades. Lower arm short as compared with other animals, slightly inclined inwards (crook), seen in profile moderately straight, not bending forward or knuckling over (unsoundness), feet large, round and strong with thick pads, toes compact and with distinct arch in each toe, nails strong. The dogs must stand true, i.e., equally on all parts of the foot. **Body Trunk :** Long and muscular, the line of back slightly depressed at shoulders and slightly arched over loin, which should be short and strong, outline of belly moderately tucked up. **Hindquarters :** Rump round, full, broad ; muscles hard and plastic, hip bone or pelvis bone not too short, broad and strongly developed, set moderately sloping ; thigh bones strong, of good length and joined to pelvis at right angles ; lower thighs short in comparison with other animals ; hocks well developed and seen from behind the legs should be straight (not cow-hocked), **hind feet** smaller in bone and narrower than fore feet. The dog should not appear higher at quarters than at shoulders. **Stern :** Set on fairly high, strong and tapering, but not too long and not too much curved nor carried too high. **Coat and Skin :** Short, dense and smooth, but strong. The hair on the underside of tail coarse in texture, skin loose and supple. Any **colour.** No white except spot on breast. Nose and sinal should be black. In red dogs a red nose is permissible, but not desirable. In chocolates and dapples the nose may be brown or flesh-coloured. In dapples large spots of colour are undesirable, and the dog should be evenly dappled all over. **Weight :** Heavy-weight dogs not exceeding 25 lb. ; heavy-weight bitches not exceeding 23 lb. Light-weight dogs not exceeding 21 lb. ; light-weight bitches not exceeding 19 lb. **Faults :** In general appearance weak or deformed, too high or too low to the ground ; ears set on too high or too low ; eyes too prominent ; muzzle too short or pinched, neither undershot nor overshot ; forelegs too much crooked or with hare or Terrier feet, or flat spread toes (flat-footed), out at elbows ; body too much dip behind the shoulders ; loins weak or too much arched ; chest too flat or too short ; hindquarters weak or cowhocked and hips higher than shoulders. It is recommended that in judging **Dachshunds** the above-mentioned negative points (faults) should only be penalised to the extent of the values allotted to such positive points.

THE DACHSHUND

Origin and History.—In later Victorian and early Edwardian days Dachshunds were much in favour among sporting men and smart women, their eccentric appearance and plucky temperament having an irresistible appeal. Long before they became naturalised Queen Victoria had many in her extensive kennels at Windsor. Some of those presented to her soon after her marriage were highly prized, as we may infer from the memorials that were erected. On the slopes in the Home Park is a solid marble pillar set in a plinth of granite, upon which is the inscription : " Here is buried Deckel, the faithful German Dachshund of Queen Victoria, who brought him from Coburg in 1845. Died Aug. 10, 1859. Aged 15 years." The breed was then almost entirely in the hands of German and Austrian nobles, and it is strange that we should have recognised their possibilities before the German populace. Our Dachshund Club was founded in 1881, ten years before a similar body was set up in Germany, and we were also the first to exhibit them. The Kennel Club and Birmingham put on classes for them in 1873, before which date they had been exhibited among foreign dogs, described as German Badger Hounds, or Daxhounds.

Actually, they were not hounds at all, the name signifying *dachs*, a badger, and *hund*, dog. The misconception was so general that we bred for a houndy type, and it was not until the beginning of this century that Mr. J. F. Sayer embarked upon a crusade in favour of a lighter, smarter and more terrier-like dog that would conform to the German standard.

Dachshunds are used on the Continent for sport both above and under ground, doing the work either of a spaniel or a

172

Photo] [Fall

DACHSHUND (Smooth) : Champion *Firgem*, the property of Mrs. B.
Huggins of East Court, Tenterden, Kent.

DACHSHUND (Long-haired) : *Ratzmann vom Habichtshof*, Imported by
Mrs. E. S. Quick.

173

terrier. The late Mr. Walter Winans kept a pack for driving wild boar to the guns in the forests, his experience being that they were much more suitable for the purpose than bigger dogs.

It is incontrovertible, I think, that the Basset or Dachshund form is of very wide distribution and ancient derivation. A similar type was known in ancient Egypt, and it is rather curious that the name Teckel, by which they are often called in Germany, should have the same sound as that of Tekal, one of the four dogs on the tomb of Antifaa II, near Thebes.

The Germans divide them into heavy, light and dwarf, the employment of a heavy or light dog depending entirely upon local conditions and the kind of sport. There are three varieties, the smooth, the wire-haired and the long-haired, and we also have miniatures which are small enough to enter a rabbit hole. Some of these mites were exhibited at the Kennel Club show of 1929 by Miss F. E. Dixon and Major G. Maitland Reynell. They should be under 9 lb. in weight. During the last few years the wires have come very much into prominence. The coats of these dogs should fit so closely that at a distance they look almost like smooths, but at the same time, they are frequently not so deep in the chest as the others. As I write, efforts are being made to establish the long-haired variety, which are furthered by the Long-haired Dachshund Club.

Standard Description.—In general appearance the dog is " long and low, but with compact and well-muscled body, neither crippled, cloddy nor clumsy, with bold defiant carriage of head and intelligent expression." Thus runs the opening to the standard of the Dachshund Club, which then proceeds to details. *Head.*—Head and skull are long, appearing conical when seen from above, and from a side view tapering to the point of the muzzle. The stop is not pronounced, and the skull should be slightly arched in profile and appearing neither too broad nor too narrow. The eyes should be of medium size, oval and set obliquely, dark in colour, except in the case of chocolates, which may be lighter, and in dapples one or both wall eyes are permissible. Ears should be broad, of moderate length and well rounded, relatively well back,

175

high and well set on, lying close to the cheek, and very mobile. The jaw should be neither too square nor snipy, but strong, with the lips tightly stretched, fairly covering the lower jaw. *Body.*—The neck should be sufficiently long, muscular, clean, with no dewlap, slightly arched in the nape, running in graceful lines into the shoulders, and carried well up and forward. Shoulder blades must be long, broad and set on sloping. The chest should be very oval with ample room for the heart and lungs, with deep and well sprung-out ribs towards the loins. The breast-bone should be prominent. The body must be long and muscular, the line of the back being slightly depressed at the shoulders and slightly arched over the loin, which should be short and strong. The outline of the belly must be moderately tucked up. Rump round, full, broad; muscles hard and plastic. The hip-bone or pelvis bone must not be too short; it must be broad, strongly developed and set moderately slop-

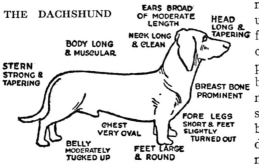

THE DACHSHUND

ing. Thigh-bones should be strong, of good length, and joined to the pelvis at right angles; lower thighs being short in comparison with other animals. Hocks well developed, not cow-hocked. The dog should not appear higher at the quarters than at the shoulders. The stern should be set on fairly high, strong and tapering, but should not be too long and not be too much curved nor carried too high. *Legs.*—The forelegs must be very short, in proportion to the size, and strong in bone. The upper arm should be of equal length with, and at right angles to, the shoulder blade; elbows lying close to the ribs, but moving freely up to the shoulder blades. The lower arm must be short as compared with other animals, slightly inclined inwards (crook), seen in profile moderately straight, not bending forward or knuckling over. *Feet.*—The feet should be large, round and strong, with thick pads. Toes must be compact and with a distinct arch in each toe ; nails strong. The hind feet should be smaller in bone and narrower than the forefeet. Dogs must stand true—i.e. equally on all parts of the foot. *Coat.*—The coat should be short, dense and smooth, but strong. The hair on the underside of the tail must be coarse in texture. Skin loose and supple. *Colour.*—Any colour. No white, except a spot on the breast. Nose and nails black. In red dogs a red nose is permissible but not desirable. In chocolates and dapples the nose may be brown or flesh-coloured. In dapples large spots of colour are undesirable, and the dog should be evenly dappled all over. *Weight.*—Heavyweight, dogs, not exceeding 25 lb. ; bitches, not exceeding 23 lb. Lightweight, dogs, not exceeding 21 lb. ; bitches, not exceeding 19 lb.

THE DACHSHUND

In spite of the fact that the Dachshund has a German name, he is not by any stretch of imagination a German dog, as the breed can claim to have been with us for over 2,000 years, and even if he has been altered slightly in appearance, his predecessors were known in Assyria and Egypt long before Germany existed.

At one period dogs long in body, with short bandy legs and large ears, were used in Central Europe against badgers and foxes, and found suitable for the work. These are presumed to be the dogs from which our present Dachshunds have been bred.

The Dachshund is a sporting little fellow, and if used against a badger can not only locate the underground brock, but worry him or drive him into his innermost earth, and hold him there until dug out.

They are also suitable animals for driving deer, as they are able to penetrate the densest undergrowth, and even if they work slowly they have the benefit of more success on account of not overrunning or frightening their quarry. As water-dogs they are wonderful, and in many respects rival the otter hound, and various packs of Dachshunds have been used with success against the wild boar.

Some years ago these dogs were nicknamed Sausage Dogs, and reference was made to them being sold by the yard. Still, such humoristic comments only assisted the breed to greater popularity, as their entertaining personality, due to their quaint appearance, helped them on the ladder of fame.

Their introduction to these shores dates from the period when Queen Victoria was presented with a team from Germany, and from that date further importations were brought in by various canine authorities, who were keen on popularising them; in fact, so much has been done to

DACHSHUND

improve the breed that today the best Dachshunds bred are those from Great Britain.

The head should be long, with a conical appearance from above, and from a side view, tapering to the side of the muzzle, wedge-shaped; eyes medium size, oval, and obliquely set, with sharp clear expression; nose black, but spotted or flesh-coloured noses are allowed in the dabble and liver-and-tan varieties; ears set moderately high, and hanging close to the cheeks, yet mobile; body long and muscular; chest deep and oval, allowing ample room for heart and lungs; back level; hair should be short and close as possible, and although smooth and glossy, should be capable of resisting the touch if stroked the wrong way; skin, although fitting close to the body, yet should be elastic and tough.

Photo]

A LONG-HAIRED DACHSHUND.

[K.N.A.

In their native Germany Dachshunds are used as their name implies to hunt badgers, their curiously shaped front feet being specially adapted for digging. The dog shown in the picture is seen with its owner, Fräulein Friedl Czepa, of Vienna, who is said to have paid £250 for it to a London dealer.

[Photo]

A NOTED GERMAN BREED.

[Sport and General

There are three types of Dachshund—the smooth, the wire-coated, and the long-haired, all of which are extremely intelligent and make excellent companions. Here are three smooth-coated members of a famous kennel "Kailora" "Karzaire", and "Karzador", the property of Miss F. E. Dixon.

THE LONG-HAIRED VARIETY OF THE GERMAN BADGER DOG.

Long-haired Dachshunds have been known in Germany for well over a hundred years, but are still not as popular as the short-coated variety. Two distinguished dogs are shown in the picture, Miss K. E. Allinson's "Kalje of Bromholm" and "Gamester of Bromholm".

Photo]   [Hugh D. Martineau.
GOOD COMPANIONS.
The Dachshund is good company, gentle and faithful, as well
as being one of the best "guards" among the smaller dogs.

KEEPING THEM DRY.

Dogs have a great aversion to rain. The owner of these two Dachshunds, in wet weather, dresses his dogs in mackintoshes.

[Paddo]

[Fox Popper.

THE SMOOTH DACHSHUND.
This breed has gradually become more and more popular in Britain. The above are typical specimens, showing their remarkable ears and shortness of leg.

THE BADGER-DOG AT WORK.

"Dachshund" means literally "badger-dog", since it was for
digging badgers that he was first bred. The above picture shows
him in the early days at various stages of his task.

DACHSHUNDS OF YORE.

Another quaint old print, valuable chiefly for showing the
great likeness between the Dachshund of three centuries ago
and his modern descendant.

186

OF HISTORICAL INTEREST.

Some of the old stamp of Dachshund were much more of Terrier type than those of to-day, and many resembled the Basset Hound.

A FINE TYPE OF DACHSHUND OF SOME YEARS AGO.

Dachshund (*Smooth*).—Although very few people realize it, there are no fewer than six varieties of Dachshund : The Smooth, the original variety from which all the others have been made ; colour black-and-tan, red, chocolate or dappled. The Wire-haired, probably made by a cross with a Scottie; colour: black-and-tan, reddish and brindle. The Long-haired variety, probably a cross with some Spaniel breed. These are said to be excellent for all kinds of hunting. The coats are smooth on the back, with beautiful feathering under the body, legs and tail. Colour usually black-and-tan or red. The Miniature Smooth-coated, which should exactly resemble their big brethren. Weight, in this country, under 10 lb ; in Germany somewhat less. The Miniature Long-haired, which should exactly resemble the ordinary ones, except in size, which is as in the Smooths; and the Rabbit Dog. The history of the Dachshund is a very long one and they seem to be descended from a short-legged, long-backed race of dogs which existed in Egypt at a very early date. There is a statue of one of the early kings seated with three dogs round him. The one between his feet is a long dog, bearing the name "Tekal", which looks as if the German name of "Teckel" (by which they are usually known there), had come from it.

All down the ages there are occasional references in European history to small hounds, which were undoubtedly the family from which the Dachshund evolved. The Goblin tapestries show a very dachshund-like dog at work.

Although the Dachshund is the national dog of Germany and they were but sparsely represented here, Britain had a specialist club for the breed many years before they had one in the former country. Queen Victoria owned one or two Dachshunds, and such names as Mudie and Millais are among those of the earliest breeders in England. Mr. John Sayer, one of our most respected judges, was for many years the breeder and importer of many good dogs. Next come such men as Mr. Woodhead and Mr. Lever, who jointly imported a number of dogs, the most notable of these, perhaps, being 'Brandesburton Filius", a great little dog, who did so much towards improving the breed, bringing back the vigour and grace of the Terrier.

THREE NOTED DOGS.
"Festus" Waldman", and "Schlupferle" were three important dogs at the end of the nineteenth century.

"MR. WEBSTER" AND THE COUNTESS.
A great lover of animals, the Countess of Northesk is here seen with her favourite Dachshund, "Mr. Webster".

One can only mention here a few of the great names of history, and "Brandesburton Filius" stands right out as a landmark. It was a funny little dog, not really beautiful to look at, but its owner saw that it was what was needed here. This dog did not become a champion, but its work will carry its name down to posterity as no title could ever do.

The wonder dog Ch. "Honeystone", a son of his, was the sire of so many champions that one loses count of them. The curious fact is that it

dog, the friend replied, "That is a Dachshund, not a dog". They are very clever too. Not only do they quickly learn the ordinary dog tricks; they are dogs who really think. If a Dachshund is shut up it will spend hours trying patiently to find a way out. There was a Dachshund once which taught itself to open all the patent fasteners on the kennel gates and, having let itself out, would then go across to the pen where the bitches lived and open their gate, which had quite a different fastening

Photo]　　　　　　　　　　　　　　　　　　　　　　　　　　　　　　　　　[E.N.A.
FROM AUSTRIA.
There is something very intriguing about the young Dachshund, as will be seen by this photo from Vienna of a typical mother and her family.

sired far more bitch champions than dogs. Then comes the reign of "Remegan Max", the wonderful red dog imported by Mr. Dunlop, who did much for the breed by importing many good dogs, including Ch. "Faust v. Forstenberg". Most of the great German families have sent members here from time to time. Luitpoldesheim, Asbecks, Forstenberg, Weidmannsfreud, Berkenschloss, Neumarkt, Webber, are among the number.

In character the Dachshund is most lovable and intelligent. His qualities are so highly placed by the German race that once, it is said, when a man spoke to his friend about his Dachshund as a

They are marvellous diggers, and it is next to impossible to keep them in runs, such as are used for Terriers; one has to sink the wire below the ground because they tunnel under ordinary fences. A dog has been known to tunnel right under a four-foot kennel to get out.

The type of the Dachshund has altered considerably as, following on the German lines, they have become very much lighter, though something has been sacrificed in the way of bone strength. When first the Dachshund came to this country it was a very clumsy and inelegant dog, owning huge floppy ears and weighing anything up to

ARISTOCRATS.
Two handsome Dachshunds belonging to Mrs. Basil Huggins.

30 lb., whereas now the popular weight is round about 17 lb.

The standard in this country varies very little from that accepted in Germany; in fact, our list of points is practically copied from theirs. Most judges here prefer stronger hindquarters than the German judges, who lay rather more stress on immense length of body, but in all essentials we strive for the same thing—a real working dog.

Although, unfortunately, Dachshunds are not much worked in England, all the chief breeders keep work in mind when breeding, with the result that our dogs are nearly all of a type which could and would work, given the chance.

All Dachshunds will hunt a rabbit or any small quarry on scent and, when trained, will follow a trail laid for miles. The clever bitch Ch. "Foxhope" was splendid at this work—a rabbit-skin being used to lay the trail. A Colonel in India owned a bitch which went to ground with a civet cat, remaining so long underground that she was given up for dead; but she returned after thirty-six hours, bringing the cat with her, dead. Another man recounts that he was out after wild boar with his Dachshund, which got badly mauled and had to be nursed for a long while before it recovered. When it was well again it went back with its master to the same place and helped to get a boar, possibly the same one.

Dachshunds are not aggressive dogs, but once their temper is roused they will fight to the death,

disregarding pain. They are perhaps the most exclusive "one man" dog of all breeds and will, at about a year old, make up their minds once and for all who is to be master or mistress. Thenceforward they will follow that person to the end of the earth.

In Germany there are not a great many very large kennels for Dachshunds, as they are so often bred by foresters (keepers as we should call them), and when they are bred purely for show purposes they are usually bred in small numbers, having the run of the house, with a barrel and a small run in the yard.

They are quite hardy dogs but, like all other breeds, they can be made delicate by excessive pampering, overheating, and indulgence. Greedy they are, so that it is easy to spoil them; the horrible fat lazy ones, which used to be seen about so often in towns, were the result of over-indulgence with pampering. The true Dachshund is a dog who loves nothing better than to be racing about all day.

One great attraction of the breed is that they do well in any climate—even in the Plains of India. They revel in heat; by reason of their short, smooth coats they do not seem to feel it.

During the war there were only about six breeders who kept the Dachshund going, one of whom was the Secretary of the club, Major Hayward, O.B.E., who had his wonderful dog Ch. "Honeystone" with him in garrison for some time.

In this breed, family features are very clearly marked, and it is interesting to watch the judging at a big show and see if one can trace the family from which each exhibit came.

One of the reasons why many people think them nervous is simply because they hate to be handled by strangers; this adds to their value as guard-dogs, as does also their large bark, which is

A NOTED CHAMPION.
Ch. "Fir Tinkergirl", one of Mrs. Huggins' famous kennel, is a well-known winner.

often more the bay of the hound than the bark of a terrier.

The Long-haired variety are, many of them, splendid water dogs and learn quickly to retrieve in water.

Some people say that they are not good whelpers, but this is untrue, and if proper care is taken of them at these times they are no more trouble than any other valuable dogs.

They usually have litters of five or six, and make splendid mothers, being very devoted to their puppies. More than once bitches have brought up puppies of other breeds very successfully.

TIMIDITY

Dachshund puppies, if confronted with a stranger and a camera, prefer, like most other puppies, to seek safety in flight.

The puppies are the merriest and most attractive little things, and make delightful pets for children. They are usually late developers, often not coming to their prime until two or even three years old, but many have been known to live to a great age. Mrs. Saunders, the well-known breeder, had a dog who lived for eighteen years. Ch. "Honeystake", too, lived to a good old age. They are not delicate, and need very little fussing. Many breeders use unheated kennels for them all the year round.

As house dogs they are good, because they do not bring dirt into the house, and once trained they are amusingly conservative in their habits, insisting on retiring to bed and having their meals at the same time every day.

OFFICAL STANDARD OF POINTS :

GENERAL APPEARANCE.—The form is compact, short-legged and long-backed, but sinewy and well muscled, with bold and defiant head carriage, and intelligent expression. The body should be neither too plump nor too slender. Height at shoulder should be half the length of the body measured from the breast-bone to the set-on of the tail, and the girth of the chest double the height at the shoulder. The length from the tip of the nose to the eyes should be equal to the length from the eyes to the base of the skull.

HEAD.—Long and conical when seen from above, in profile sharp and finely modelled. Skull neither too broad nor too narrow, only slightly arched, without prominent stop. Fore-face long and narrow, finely modelled.

LIPS.—Tightly drawn, well covering the lower jaw, neither too heavy nor too sharply cut away ; the corners of the mouth slightly marked.

MOUTH.—Wide, extending back to behind the eyes, furnished with strong teeth which should fit into one another exactly, the inner side of the upper incisors closing on the outer side of the under ones.

EYES.—Medium in size, oval, set obliquely, clear, expressive and dark in colour.

EARS.—Broad and placed relatively well back, high and well set on, lying close to the cheeks, broad, long, and very mobile.

NECK.—Sufficiently long, muscular, showing no dewlap, slightly arched at the nape, running gracefully into the shoulders, carried well up and forward.

A STUDY IN EXPRESSION.

Here are shown some charming heads of Mrs. Barr's Dachshunds. Looking at this picture there is small wonder that the Dachshunds are becoming more and more popular.

192

A CHARMING PICTURE.

Viscountess Harcourt, with her two babies, and a Smooth-haired Dachshund, their constant companion.
Dachshunds make admirable pets for children, because they are so even-tempered, kind, and reliable.

193

FOREQUARTERS.—Muscular, with deep chest. Shoulders long and broad, set obliquely, lying firmly on well-developed ribs. Muscles hard and plastic. Breast-bone prominent, extending so far forward as to show depressions on both sides. Upper arm the same length as the shoulder-blade, jointed at right angles to the shoulder, well boned and muscled, set on close to the ribs but moving freely as far as the shoulder-blade. Lower arm comparatively short, inclined slightly inwards, solid and well muscled.

well muscled. Hocks set wide apart, strongly ben and, seen from behind, the legs should be straight.—

FEET.—Broad and large, straight or turned slightly outwards ; the hind feet smaller and narrower than the fore. Toes close together and with a distinct arch to each toe. Nails strong. The dog must stand equally on all parts of the foot.

TAIL.—Set on fairly high, not too long, tapering and without too marked a curve. Not carried too high.

Photo]   [Dorien Leigh.

AN INTERLUDE.

The serious business of learning seems to be endangered by the accidental meeting of a schoolboy and a Dachshund puppy Young Dachshunds are such playful little fellows.

BODY (Trunk).—Long and well muscled, the back showing oblique shoulders and short and strong pelvic region. Ribs very oval, deep between the forelegs and extending far back. Loins short, strong, and broad. The line of the back slightly depressed over the shoulders and slightly arched over the loins, with the outline of the belly moderately tucked up.

HINDQUARTERS.—Rump round, full, broad, with muscles well modelled and plastic. Pelvis bone not too short, broad, strongly developed and set obliquely. Thigh bone strong, of good length and jointed to the pelvis at right angles. Second thigh short, set at right angles to the upper thigh,

COAT.—Soft, smooth, and glossy.

COLOUR. — Black - and - tan, dark - brown with lighter shadings, dark-red, light-red, dappled, tiger-marked or brindled.

NOSE AND NAILS.—In black-and-tan, red and dappled dogs these should be black ; in chocolates they are often brown.

WEIGHT AND SIZE.—The same as Long-haired Dachshund (which see).

Dachshund (Long-haired).—This is an old fixed sub-variety of the "Teckel", though his origin is by no means clear. Some say he used to do the groundwork for the Salukis in Abyssinia,

194

[Photo] WHAT CAN IT BE! [Fall.

Two youthful smooth Dachshunds, the property of Mrs. Huggins, are here seen displaying an alert interest in something off-stage. The keen expression is very typical.

[Photo] A CHAMPION AND HIS FRIEND. [Fall.

A charming study of a dog and bitch belonging to Miss D. Spurrier. They are "Saucy Sue" and Ch. "Dicker von Kornerpark" an attractive pair, and representative of the breed.

195

while others profess to trace the breed to Egypt. A further opinion has been expressed that the breed is directly descended from the Basset Hound of La Vendée.

There is some doubt as to whether the breed is original or something developed. According to Dr. Fritz Engelmann, who wrote his well-known book on the Dachshund in 1925, every breed has more or less the blood of some other breed in it, and the Dachshund, in his opinion, has a large strain of Spaniel blood.

In 1812, mention is made of the Long-haired variety in Germany, and in 1820 the Long-haired Dachshund is referred to by Dietrich aus dem Winkell ; and Dr. Reichenbach in 1836 enumerated all the varieties, and this is especially interesting as some of them are still in vogue at the present time.

The popularisation of the Long-haired Dachshund is due to some extent to Captain von Bunau of Bernberg, who wrote a book in 1882 entitled, *Dog*. He referred in that book to the hunting qualities of this breed, and gives as an instance of this an account of what happened in the course of an Archducal hunt in or about 1874. On this occasion a roebuck was badly wounded and took refuge in an impenetrable thicket, which even normally strong dogs could scarcely penetrate. After holding a council of war, the hunters put their last hope in "Manne", a Long-haired Dachshund, which was brought from a neighbouring

Photo] KEEPING OUT OF THE COLD. [B.I.P.
In April 1934 a Dachshund Show was held at Tattersall's. Our picture shows Mrs. D. W. Elliott, the well-known breeder, keeping her three entries warmly covered with a rug.

village and which, after a short search, successfully located the wounded roebuck. Captain von Bunau acquired the dog and subsequently bought a bitch and bred from them. He found them very good both at picking up scent and in groundwork, and equal to the smartest Water Spaniels in duck-hunting, owing to their assiduous and indefatigable searching and retrieving.

Persons not aware of the sporting properties of this breed, but who exercise their so-called sense of humour by referring to the Dachshund as a good family dog —because all the members of the family can stroke it at the same time, a sausage-dog, or as 'the dog that is sold by the yard"—do not know that this comparatively small dog engages in a fierce fight with an animal as vicious as the badger, and in its lair too. Dachshund means "badger dog", and this title has been well earned in Germany. Furthermore, its terrier qualities would make it useful in assisting the Otter Hounds. It combines in its small person the characteristics both of hound and terrier. Its long ears and abnormal powers of scent, and, for its size, enormous bone, prove its descent from the dog that hunts by scent. Its small size, iron courage, and anxiety to go down a hole in the ground illustrate the terrier qualities.

The characteristics of the breed demand that a Dachshund of the right size should have the maximum strength, skill, endurance, hardihood and zeal. It is these qualities, together with sureness of scent and determination and a certain obstinacy, which form the basis of the Dachshund character.

The most characteristic quality of the Dachshund is an inborn hatred of all that preys—a hatred that will not rest until the adversary has been annihilated either by its own strength or with the help of the huntsman. This will-to-kill is the father of endurance and sharpness. It is doubtless owing to the greatest curse which rests on the Dachshund, viz. their being bred in kennels and in large numbers through many generations that this "will" has been already greatly weakened.

There are more Dachshunds bred than can possibly be worked. It is a biological fact that organs which are not used grow weaker, so that the hunting impulse is growing weaker and there is an ever-increasing number of non-hunters amongst them.

The following is the official standard of points adopted by the Long-haired Dachshund Club

GENERAL APPEARANCE.—Form, colour, size and character similar in all respects to those of the Smooth Dachshund, except for the long, soft hair. The form is compact, short-legged and long, but sinewy and well muscled, with bold and defiant head carriage and intelligent expression. In spite of the shortness of the legs the body should be

neither too plump, nor so slender as to have a weasel-like appearance. Height at shoulder should be half the length of the body measured from the breast-bone to the set-on of the tail and the girth of the chest double the height at the shoulder. The length from the tip of the nose to the eyes should be equal to the length from the eyes to the base of the skull. The tail should not touch the ground when at rest, neither should the ears (i.e. the leather) extend beyond the nose when pulled to the front.

HEAD.—Long and conical when seen from above, and in profile sharp and finely modelled. Skull neither too broad nor too narrow, only slightly arched, without prominent stop Fore-face long and narrow, finely modelled.

LIPS.—Tightly drawn, well covering the lower jaw, neither too heavy nor too sharply cut away ; the corners of the mouth slightly marked.

MOUTH.—Wide, extending back to behind the eyes, furnished with strong teeth which should fit into one another exactly, the inner side of the upper incisors closing on the outer side of the under ones.

EYES.—To be medium in size, oval set obliquely, clear, expressive and dark in colour.

EARS.—Broad and placed relatively well back, high and well set on, lying close to the cheeks, broad and long, nicely feathered and very mobile.

NECK.—Sufficiently long, muscular, showing no dewlap, slightly arched at the nape, running gracefully

Photo]   FROM STYRIA.   [E.N.A.
Styria is the Dachshund's native land. Here is a Styrian lad, in national costume with his Smooth and Long-haired "Dackrels".

into the shoulders, carried well up and forward.

FOREQUARTERS.—Muscular, with deep chest. Shoulders long and broad, set obliquely, lying firmly on well-developed ribs. Muscles hard and plastic. Breast-bone prominent, extending so far forward as to show depressions on both sides. Upper arm the same length as the shoulder-blade, jointed at right angles to the shoulder, well boned and muscled, set on close to the ribs, but moving freely as far as the shoulder-blade. Lower arm comparatively short, inclined slightly inwards, solid and well muscled.

BODY (Trunk).—Long and well muscled, the back showing oblique shoulders and short and strong pelvic region. Ribs very oval, deep between the fore-legs and extending far back. Loins short, strong and broad. The line of the back slightly depressed over the shoulders and slightly arched over the loins, with the outline of the belly moderately tucked up.

HINDQUARTERS. —Rump round, full, broad, with muscles well modelled and plastic. Pelvis bone not too short, broad, strongly developed and set obliquely. Thigh-bone strong, of good length and jointed to the pelvis at right angles. Second thigh short, set at right angles to the upper thigh, well muscled. Hocks set wide apart, strongly bent and, seen from behind, the legs should be straight.

Photo]   !Fall.
A GOOD COMPANION.
Head study of "Cato of Carlisle", Mrs. Hayne's prize-winning Smooth Dachshund

FEET.—Broad and large, straight or turned slightly outwards ; the hind feet smaller and narrower than the fore. Toes close together and with a distinct arch to each toe. Nails strong. The dog must stand equally on all parts of the foot.

TAIL.—Set on fairly high, not too long, tapering and without too marked a curve. Not carried too high. Fully feathered.

COAT.—Soft and straight or slightly waved, of shining colour. Longer under the neck, the underparts of the body and particularly on the ears,

behind the legs, where it should develop into abundant feathering, and reach its greatest length on the tail, where it should form a flag. The feathering should extend to the under sides of the ears, where short hair is not desired. Too heavy a coat gives an appearance of undue plumpness and hides the outline. The coat should resemble that of an Irish Setter, giving the dog an appearance of elegance. Too much hair on the feet is ugly and useless.

COLOUR. — Black-and-tan, dark-brown with lighter shadings, dark-red, light-red, dappled, tiger-marked or brindled.

NOSE AND NAILS.—In black-and-tan, red and dappled dogs these should be black ; in chocolates they are often brown.

WEIGHT AND SIZE.—As a rule Long-haired Dachshunds are classified as follow : Lightweight up to 10 lb. for bitches and 11 lb. for dogs. Middleweight up to 17 lb. for bitches and 18 lb. for dogs. Heavyweight over 17 lb. for bitches and over 18 lb. for dogs. The lightweights are best suited to rabbit hunting; the middleweights for badger and fox drawing ; and the heavyweights for tracking, hunting larger animals and for water work. The last-named are also very useful for retrieving rabbits and waterfowl.

BREEDING.—The Long-haired Dachshund is more difficult to breed than the Smooth, as the perfect coat is more perplexing to produce. The crossing of Long-haired with Smooth or Wire-coated Dachshunds should be discouraged, since such crosses render it impossible to fix in heredity the correct type of coat. Crosses of this kind frequently result in faulty specimens or intermediate forms which are undesirable. Chance bred Long-haired Dachshunds, that is, long-haired dogs bred from smooth parents, are not uncommon and are throwbacks to long-hair blood in the pedigree. Such dogs should be used in breeding provided they conform to type and have correct coats, but only

199

PIONEERS OF THE BREED.
This is the first known picture of Wire-haired and Long-haired Dachshunds
It appeared in a book published about 1876.

in conjunction with mates which are known to be pure bred for generations; in this way new blood may be introduced.

VALUE OF POINTS.—General appearance, 15; head and skull, 10; eyes, 5; ears, 5; jaws and teeth, 10; neck, 5; forequarters, 15; forelegs 5; trunk, 10; feet, 10; hindquarters, 15; tail, 5; coat, 10. Total, 120.

The Kaninchen-teckel Club has also a standard which was laid down by a resolution of the Club at a meeting in Stuttgart in 1925. It may be said that the British and German standards are very much alike, although, if anything, the German standard, so far as some of the faults are concerned is slightly stricter.

Colonel Harrison, who first became interested in the breed in 1921, had several well-known dogs in his kennels in Somerset, including Ch. "Jesko von der Humboldtshöhe", and a bitch he imported from Germany, "Vossa von Bergwald" which won a Challenge Certificate at Cruft's Show the first time she was shown in this country.

Colonel W. G. Bedford was one of the first in this country to own a Long-haired Dachshund, as in 1924 he purchased "Hengist of Armadale". He then imported "Elfe von Fels" which, before leaving Germany

had been mated to "Stropp von der Windburg", and she produced in this litter Ch. "Rufus of Armadale", a winner of several Challenge Certificates and prizes and a well-known sire; and Ch. "Rose of Armadale", a successful show bitch.

Mrs. L. S Bellamy also established a successful kennel from which many winners have sprung. One was Ch. "Chloe of Armadale", a beautiful brindle, one of whose litters secured close on one hundred prizes. Ch. "Michael von Walder", a very beautiful red dog, the property of Mr. H. Hartley Russell, was also bred by her and was one of the litter referred to.

One should also mention Mrs. Raymond Reade in Suffolk, whose kennel includes Ch. "Captain of Armadale", a dark-red brindle; and Mrs Violet Ryecroft, who had many successes with the offspring of "Cinderella of Armadale", which came from Colonel Bedford's kennel, including "Bartonbury Vesta", the winner of many prizes and two Challenge Certificates; Mrs. Smith Rewse of the Primrose Patch kennels, in conjunction with her brother, Sir Beauchamp St. John, K.C.I.E., C.B.E.; Miss Ursula Still, owner of "Diana von Walder", a notable red brindle bitch, winner of several prizes and a Challenge Certificate, and "Hugo von Walder" a brother; Mrs. Midwood, owner of "Daffodil of Dilworth", a winner of Challenge Certificates; Miss Allison, Miss Sturt; the Dowager Countess of Cranbrook; and the Hon. Mrs. Parsons.

GOOD-NATURED
The charming disposition of the Dachshund is well expressed in the eyes of "Ferdinand" above which is of Austrian origin. Note the "feathers" effect of the ears.

Dachshund (*Miniature*).—The German dwarf or Rabbit Teckel, commonly known in this country as the Miniature Dachshund, is a comparatively recent importation, and until a very few years ago it was practically unknown in England. The breed was started in Germany about the year 1900 with the object of producing a Dachshund of the smallest possible proportions, to enable it to get into the narrowest rabbit burrows ; hence the name Rabbit Teckel.

It was uphill work at first. Dwarf Pinschers and Black-and-tan Terriers were used, type and character being sacrificed to the main object, viz. small size. Having achieved the desired size, it was then necessary to secure a dog that would go to ground, and one that displayed true Dachshund type and character.

The dog which in those days had most influence on the breed was called "Zwerg v. Barrach," of the Staffelstein Kennel. The Kaninchen-teckel Club was formed in 1905, with thirty-four members, and the dogs were used instead of ferrets, and also to put rabbits up out of thick undergrowth. In many instances they were used successfully against foxes, and some have been known to tackle a badger.

Black-and-tans were favoured, as were also the reds, who were much less distinguishable from the ground in autumn, and more liable to be confused with rabbits. All these three coats are bred in Germany, but the original Smooths seem the most popular.

The Kaninchen-teckel Club only registers dogs measuring a fraction over 11 ins. or less round the chest. They also register Dwarf Teckels, whose minimum chest measurement is 13 ins. and maximum weight 8 lb.

The best-known kennels in Germany were originally the v. Sonnenstein, v. Hexentanzplatz, Harras, and Hainichen. They were quickly followed by the Fleesensee, v. d. Jeetzel, v. Hoehlenkampf, v. Eulengebirge, Fehmarn, and

[*Photo*] FAITHFULNESS. [*E.N.A.*]
A head study of a curly Dachshund. Note the kindness and faithfulness expressed in his calm brown eyes.

others. The Miniature type is now firmly established, and there is little fear of throw-backs to large size, but there is still room for improvement in general type and soundness.

With a view to popularizing this breed in England Miss F. E. Dixon, Mrs. Howard and Major Maitland Reynell brought over a batch of these little dogs about the year 1929, and the two latter have imported others since then. Several other Dachshund breeders have also taken up this fascinating variety.

Up to date the Kennel Club do not recognize the Miniatures as a separate variety. There is no Club or standard of points other than the official Smooth or Long-haired standard. Classes confined to Miniatures, generally for all types of coats, have been put on at the principal shows, with weights restricted to 10 lb.

The German custom of measuring the chest circumference has not been adopted here.

As will have been noted, slightly heavier dogs are allowed in England than in Germany, but the desired object is, by careful selective breeding, to produce perfect replicas of the best specimens of the breed. A 10 lb. dog is not too big to go to ground, and it has been observed that the smallest specimens in each litter are more leggy and less typical in head than their larger brethren.

Major Maitland Reynell has the best-known kennel of Miniature Long-hairs in this country, and his "Hallodri v. Fleesensee" is a well-nigh perfect little model of a Long-hair. Another celebrity in this kennel is "Zwergin Ariel v. Himmel", whose chief claim to fame is that it was born in the aeroplane coming over from Germany, when its mother was only six weeks gone in whelp. Its adult weight is only just over 5 lb.

It is doubtful if there are any Miniature Wire-hairs in this country, and judging from those seen in Germany in 1933, it will be some time yet before breeders will be able to produce a dog which resembles the genuine article.

Undoubtedly the best-known Miniature Smooth sire in England is Mrs. Howard's "Kleinkurio". Born in quarantine in 1929, and bred by Miss Dixon, it was sired by "Fips-Harras", out of "Mara Harras". Its weight at first was 6¼ lb. His daughter, "Mignonne of Seale," out of Mrs. Howard's imported bitch, "Hexe v. Duesternsee."

Photo] THREE MONTHS OLD. *[S. & G.*
An interesting litter of prize-winning pups belonging to Miss P. Seton-Buckley. These puppies are the Wire-haired Dachshund variety.

is recognized to be the best Miniature in this country, having beaten every Miniature she has met in the show ring, with the one exception of its mother, at the time of writing. In addition, it has also won in Variety class at Championship and Open Shows. Its weight is 9½ lb. and chest measurement 15½ ins.

The demand for typical, well-bred stock is already far in excess of the supply, and all that is required to help these fascinating little dogs—which combine intensely sporting characteristics with small size and attractive appearance—to become more widely known is a recognized club and separate registration.

Dachshund (*Wire-haired*). — Wire-Haired Dachshunds were originally bred in Germany, and one of the first shows at which one appeared was the Berlin Show in 1888. They were first obtained by mating a Smooth-haired Dachshund and a Rough-haired Pinscher, but although this gave the rough coat the head was rather short and small. Later it was discovered that the Dandie Dinmont had an excellent Dachshund pose, so that they were used for mating with the Smooth-haired Dachshund and a much better result was obtained. The Dandie can still be traced in some of the Wire-haired Dachshunds, especially about the head when the coat is long and silky.

In Germany they are bred for hunting badgers, stags and wild boar. They are keen, courageous sportsmen, with very good noses, deep voices, and are quite untiring. Their quick intelligence, strong bodies and short limbs, make them most suitable for field hunting, and in England they are used for rabbiting, ratting, etc., with great success.

Photo] *[Sport and General.*
FATHER AND SON.
"Hannes von der Abtshecke" was a double grand champion of Germany, and "Kadett of How" has also won prizes. The dogs belong to Mrs. W. Buisfield and Mr. H. A. Fischer

Photo] [L.N.A.

A CANINE HELPER.

"Astra", a Miniature Long-haired Dachshund, entered for Tattersall's Dachshund Dog Show, is assisting a juvenile programme seller.

They are very much a "one-man" dog, and having attached themselves to one person, as far as they are concerned no one else exists. They are extremely clean little animals, very easy to house train, excellent house dogs, very sensitive to rebuke or unkindness, but at the same time extremely determined and liking, if possible, to get their own way. Their short coats make them easy to keep clean and they have one great advantage that, when wet, or indeed at any time, their coats never smell.

The Wire-haired Dachshund was little known in this country until about 1927. In that year the Wire-haired Dachshund Club was started, some of the chief originators being Lady Kitty Ritson, Mrs. Schuster, Mrs. Howard, and Air Vice-Marshal Sir Charles Lambe, and two classes were guaranteed, viz. : Open Dog and Open Bitch at the Veterinary College Show. From that time to the present the Wire-haired Dachshund has made

Photo]   [E.N.A.
A BEVY OF BEAUTIES.
Fräulein Maria Paudler, particularly well known as the star of the German Talkie version of "Waltzes from Vienna", is a great dog-lover. The dog on the left is a Long-haired Dachshund.

tremendous strides in England both in numbers and in the breeding.

The Wire-haired Club started an Open Show at Tattersall's in 1932, and in 1933 was joined by the Southern Smooths and Long-haired Clubs. Major Ilgner, one of the oldest and most experienced German judges, judged the Wires and he was delighted with them.

The first dog to become a champion in England was Ch. "Fritzle von Paulinenberg", born 1925, an imported dog owned by the late Mrs. Rattee and afterwards by Mrs. Allan. Another imported dog to become a champion was "Dictator Ditmarsia", born 1928. and owned by Mrs. Mitchell.

The first English-bred dog to become a champion was "Achsel", born 1929 and owned by Miss Theo Watts. Ch. "Achsel" was awarded best Wire-haired dog or bitch by Major Ilgner at the Open Joint Show at Tattersall's, 1933. also by "Myrhea Fokker" at Cruft's, 1933. He sired Ch. "Amelia", owned by Mrs. Blandy, born 1931. Ch. "Anneta", born 1929, bred and owned by Mrs. Blandy, was the first Wire-haired bitch bred in England to become a champion. Ch. "Brita of Tavistone", born

Photo]   [Sport and General.
IN THE HANDS OF THE JUDGE.
The picture of the Countess Reventlow (of Denmark) judging Wire-haired Dachshunds at a Kennel Club Show. Notice the dappled colouring of the dog furthest from the camera.

A CHARMING LOT.
Miss Pamela Howard, with her mother's extremely attractive Miniature Dachshunds, at the Club's Jubilee Show at Tattersall's, London, in 1935.

205

1925, was an imported bitch owned by the late Mrs. Rattee. There was one other English-bred bitch, Ch. "Diana of Tavistone", owned by Mmes. Howard and Schuster, but she died when only two and a half years old and was a great loss to the breed.

"KLEINKURIO".
Said to be the smallest toy Dachshund in the world.

The chief features as adopted by the Wire-haired Dachshund Club in the main are similar to those of the Smooth-haired variety already given, with the exception, of course, of the coat.

Apart from jaw, eyebrows, and ears, the whole body is covered with a completely even, short, thick, rough coat, but with finer, shorter hairs everywhere distributed between the coarser hairs, which resembles that of the German spiky-haired Pointer. There should be a beard on the chin. The eyebrows are bushy. On the ears the hair is shorter than on the body; quite smooth, but nevertheless in conformity with the rest of the coat. It is a fault if the texture of the hair is soft, if too short or too long anywhere, if it sticks out irregularly in all directions, or if curling or wavy. All colours are admissible. White patches on the chest, though allowable, are not desirable. The colour of the nose and nails should be black.

Photo]   [Ralph Robinson.
"MIGNONNE OF SEALE".
An adult example of the Dachshund in miniature. It is the property of Major Howard.

Photo]   [Ralph Robinson.
DACHSHUNDS IN MINIATURE.
Mrs. M. Howard has a noted kennel of Miniature Dachshunds; here a bitch is seen with her puppies.

THREE GOOD TYPES.

It is not often that such fine specimens of the Wire-haired variety are seen, as those shown above. That in the centre is "Diana of Tavistone", the property of Mrs. M. Howard. That below shows "Kingswalden Flute". The Wire-haired Dachshund is often quite different from the smooth type, sometimes giving the impression of being a distinct variety.

207

THE DACHSHUND   Ruben von de Jowitt

Everyone is familiar with the Dachshund and, although it is not prepossessing, the fact remains that the dog is one of the most popular breeds ever imported into this country.

The Dachshund, as is generally known, originated in Germany, and one of its ancestors was undoubtedly an Otter Hound. Proof of this contention is revealed on comparing the breeds.

There are three main types exhibited to-day : the Smooth, the Wire, and the Long-haired in the larger dogs, apart from the Miniature variety, which is mainly Smooth-coated.

THE DACHSHUND   TANTIVEY MATILDA

THE DACHSHUND   Ch. Achsel

A LITTER OF " NAZEING " SMOOTHS

THE DACHSHUND

211

THE DACHSHUND   CHEPPING PUMPERNICKEL

THE DACHSHUND

A Litter of Long-coated
" Knowltons "

THE DACHSHUND

RACIAL CHARACTERISTICS OF THE DACHSHUND

(According to a resolution of the German Teckel Club E.V. Headquarters, Berlin, at a General Meeting held at Stuttgart on May 8th, 1925.)

1.—GENERAL FEATURES

FORMATION OF BODY.—HEAD : Viewed from above or from the side, it should taper uniformly to the tip of the nose, and should be clean cut and show much character. The skull only slightly arched, and should slope gradually without stop (the less the stop the more typical) to the finely formed slightly arched muzzle. The bridge bones over the eyes should be strongly prominent.

The nasal cartilage (this refers to the cartiliganeous portion beyond the actual skeleton— *i.e.*, bone), and ridge long and narrow, lips tightly stretched, well covering the lower jaw, but neither deep nor taper-like, corner of the mouth not very marked. Jaws widely extensible, joint of lower with upper jaw should be in a vertical line behind the eyes, with strongly developed bones and teeth.

Powerful canines, closely biting together, and the outer side of the lower front teeth should tightly touch the inner side of the upper.

EYES : Medium size oval, situated at the sides, with an energetic, but nevertheless friendly expression, but not piercing. Colour, lustrous dark to black-brown for all varieties. Wall (fish or pearl) eyes in the case of grey or dapple-coloured dogs, are not faulty, but are not desirable.

EARS : Should be set near the top of the head, and not too far forward, and beautifully rounded, not narrow pointed or folded. They should be in constant movement ; and the forward edge should be closely in contact with the cheek.

NECK : Sufficiently long, muscular, clean cut, not showing any dewlap on the throat, slightly arched in the neck, extending in a graceful line between the shoulders, and carried erect.

FRONT : To endure the arduous exertion underground, the front must be correspondingly muscular, compact, deep, long and broad.

IN DETAIL.—(*a*) SHOULDER BLADE : Long, broad, obliquely and firmly placed upon the fully developed thorax, muscled with hard and supple muscles. (*b*) UPPER ARM : Of the same length as the shoulder-blade, and at right angles to the latter, strong of bone and hard of muscle, lying close to the ribs, but freely movable. (*c*) FOREARM : This is short in comparison with other breeds, slightly turned inwards, in front and on the outside muscled with hard but supple muscles, and on the inside and at the back, the tendons should be tightly stretched. (*d*) JOINT BETWEEN FOREARM AND FOOT (WRISTS) : These are closer together than the shoulder joints, so that the front does not appear of uniform width. (*e*) PAWS : Full, broad in front, and a trifle inclined outwards, compact, well-arched toes, and with tough pads. (*f*) TOES : There are five of these, though four only are in use. They should be close together, with a pronounced curvature, and provided on top with strong nails, and underneath with tough toe-pads.

(*a*) TRUNK : The breast-bone should be strong, and so prominent in front that on either side a shallow depression (dimple) should be apparent. When viewed from the front the thorax should appear oval and should extend downward to the mid-point of the forearm, sometimes styled knee. The cavity enclosed by the ribs full and oval, and when seen from above or on one side full volumed, so as to allow by its ample capacity complete development of heart and lungs. Well ribbed up, and gradually merging into the line of the abdomen. If the length is correct, and also the anatomy of the shoulder and upper arm, the front legs should, when viewed from one side, cover the lowest point of the breast-line. (*b*) ABDOMEN : This should be slightly drawn up. The whole trunk should in general be long and fully muscled. The back, with sloping shoulders and short, rigid pelvis, should lie in the straightest possible line between the withers and very slightly arched loins, these latter being short, rigid and broad.

HINDQUARTERS.—(*a*) The croup long, round, full, robustly muscled, but supple, only slightly sinking towards the tail. (*b*) Pelvic bones not too short, sufficiently strongly developed, and moderately sloping. (*c*) Thigh bone robust and of good length, and set at right angles to the pelvic bone. (*d*) Hind legs robust and well muscled, with well-rounded buttocks. (*e*) Knee joint broad and strong. (*f*) Calf bone. This, in comparison with other breeds, is short; it should be perpendicular to the thigh bone and strongly muscled. (*g*) The bones at the base of the foot should present a flat appearance, with a strongly prominent hock and a wide Achilles tendon. (*h*) Central foot bones. These should be long, movable towards the calf bone, slightly bent towards the front, but perpendicular. (*i*) Hind paws. Four compactly closed and beautifully arched toes, as in the case of the front paws. The whole foot should be posed equably on the ball and not merely on the toes; nails short. In contrast to the front, the hindquarters viewed from behind should be of completely equal length.

TAIL: Set in continuation with the spine, and extending without very pronounced curvature, and should not be too gaily carried.

GENERAL APPEARANCE: Low to ground, short legged, long in the body, but with compact figure and robust muscular development; with sprightly defiant carriage of the head and an intelligent expression. In spite of his short limbs, in comparison with his length of body, he should appear neither crippled, awkward, cramped in his capacity for movement, or weasel-like.

QUALITIES: He should be clever, lively and courageous to the point of rashness, persevering in his work both above and below ground; with collective intelligence well developed. His build and disposition qualify him especially for hunting his prey below ground. Added to this, his keenness for sport, good nose, sonorous voice, and small size, render him specially suited for field hunting. His figure and his fine nose qualify him especially before most other breeds of sporting dogs for tracking.

2.—SPECIAL CHARACTERISTICS OF THE VARIOUS KINDS OF DACHSHUNDS

The Teckel is bred with three varieties of hair: (A) Short-haired; (B) Rough-haired; (C) Long-haired. All three varieties should conform to the characteristics already specified. The long and short-haired are old, long-prevailing varieties, but into the rough-haired Teckel the blood of other breeds has been purposely introduced; but, nevertheless, in breeding him the greatest stress must be placed on conformity to the general Teckel type.

The following are applicable to the three types in particular :—

(A) SHORT-HAIRED DACHSHUND.—HAIR: Short, thick, shining; no bald patches. Special faults are: Too fine or thin hair, leathery ears, bald patches, or too coarse or too thick hair in general.

TAIL: Gracefully carried but not too richly haired, long bristles on the underside is a sign of a patch of strong-growing hair; it is not a fault. A brush tail is a fault, as is also a partly or wholly hairless tail.

COLOUR OF HAIR, NOSE, AND NAILS.—(*a*) MONO COLOUR TECKELS: This class includes red, red-yellow, yellow, including those with black streaks. Nevertheless, a clean colour is preferable, and red is to be considered more desirable than red-yellow or yellow. Also strongly black-streaked dogs belong to this class, and not to the variety coloured. Nose and nails black; red is admissable, but not desirable.

(*b*) BI-COLOURED TECKELS: These comprise deep black or brown, grey or white, each with rust-brown or yellow marks over the eyes, on the sides of the face and underlip, on the inner edge of the ear, front, breast, inside and behind the front legs, on the paws and around the ankles, and from there to about one-half or one-third of the length of tail on the underside. NOSE AND NAILS : In the case of black dogs, black ; for grey or white dogs, grey or even flesh colour, but the last named colour is not desirable ; in the case of white dogs, black (*i.e.*, nose and nails) is to be preferred. For mono-colour dogs, and for bi-coloured (white not being one of the colours) no white is desirable, but in solitary small patches it is not exactly disqualifying.

(*c*) DAPPLE AND STRIPED TECKELS : The colour of the dapple Teckel is a clear brownish or greyish colour, or even white ground, with dark irregular patches (large areas of one colour not desirable) of dark-grey, brown, red-yellow, or black colour. It is desirable that neither the light nor the dark colour should predominate. The colour of the striped Teckel is red or yellow, with a darker streaking. NOSE AND NAILS : As for mono and bi-coloured.

(B) ROUGH-HAIRED DACHSHUND.—The general appearance the same as that of the short-haired, but, without being long in the legs, it is permissable for the body to be somewhat higher off the ground.

HAIR : With the exception of the jaw, eye-brows, ears, the whole body is covered with a completely even (might be translated " with a completely even short thick rough coat, but with finer shorter hairs everywhere distributed between the coarser hairs,") wool-permeated undercoat, close lying ; and short, thick rough coat, which resembles that of the German spiky-haired Pointer. There should be a beard on the chin. The eyebrows are bushy. On the ears the hair is shorter than on the body ; quite smooth, but nevertheless in conformity with the rest of the coat.

TAIL : Robust, as thickly haired as possible, gradually diminishing, and without a tuft. The general arrangement of the hair should be such that the rough-haired Dachshund when seen from a distance should resemble the smooth-haired. Faulty is it if the texture of the hair is soft in general, or if it is too short or too long in any particular place, or if it sticks out irregularly in all directions, or if curling or wavy ; a flag tail is also objectionable.

COLOUR OF HAIR, NOSE AND NAILS : All colours are admissible. White patches on the chest, though allowable, are not desirable.

(C) LONG-HAIRED DACHSHUND.—The distinctive characteristic differentiating this class from the rough-haired Dachshund is alone the long silky hair.

THE HAIR : The soft, sleek shining, often slightly waved hair should be longer under the neck, on the underside of the body, and especially on the ears, and behind the legs, becoming there a pronounced feather ; the hair should attain its greatest length on the underside of the tail. The hair should fall beyond the lower edge of the ear. Short hair on this place (the ear), so-called leather ears, is not desirable. Too luxurious a coat causes the long-haired Teckel to seem coarse, and masks the type. The coat should remind one of an Irish Setter, and should give the dog an elegant appearance. Too thick hair on the paws, so-called " mops," is inelegant, and renders the animal unfit for use.

THE TAIL : Carried gracefully in prolongation of the spine ; the hair here attains its greatest length and forms a veritable flag. Faulty is it if the hair is equally long all over the body, or if it is too curly, or too scrubby, or if a flag tail is lacking, also if the hair overhangs the ear, or if there is a very pronounced parting on the back, or a vigorous growth between the toes. Colour of hair, nose and nails exactly as for the short-haired Teckel.

3.—GENERAL FAULTS

SERIOUS FAULTS : (*a*) *Faults which exclude from any commendations.*—(" Commendations " here refers to the judge's added commendations of vorzuglich—excellent, sehr gut—very good, gut—good, which are usually bestowed on prize-winners. Thus, a second prize-winner really gets the vorzuglich, as well as the first prize-winner) : Over and undershot jaws ; knuckling over ; very loose shoulders ; toes turned inwards, or too obliquely outwards ; spreading paws ; a hollow back ; a roach back ; stern higher than withers ; a receding or weak thorax.

(*b*) *Faults which exclude from a higher classification than " good "* : A weak, long-legged, or dragging figure ; body hanging between the shoulders ; a sluggish, clumsy, or waddling gait ; excessively drawn-up flanks, like those of the Greyhound ; narrow muscle ; deficient stern ; weak loins ; badly developed front or hind-quarters ; cowhocks ; bowed hind legs ; glass eyes, except for grey, dapple, and striped dogs ; a bad coat.

Light faults which, however, prevent the classification " excellent " : Ears wrongly set, sticking out, narrow or folded ; too marked a forehead ; too pointed or weak a jaw ; pincer teeth, distemper teeth ; too wide or too short a head ; goggle eyes, *glass eyes in the case of grey and dapple dogs* ; insufficiently dark eyes in the case of all species ; dewlaps ; short neck ; a swan neck ; too fine or thin hair.

NOTE.—The following resolutions of the German Teckel Club will be of interest :— 1, From and after 1926 classes shall not be separated by colour, only by texture of hair and weight. 2, Judges who display incapacity of favouritism will in future be treated with suspension. 3, The same dog may only win the " Sieger " title once in any one year.

CLUB STANDARD OF POINTS OF THE DACHSHUND

GENERAL APPEARANCE, value 10 : Long and low, but with compact and well-muscled body, neither crippled, cloddy, nor clumsy, with bold, defiant carriage of head and intelligent expression.

HEAD AND SKULL, value 9 : Long, and appearing conical when seen from above, and from a side view tapering to the point of the muzzle. Stop not pronounced and skull should be slightly arched in profile, and appearing neither too broad nor too narrow.

EYES, value 3 : Medium in size, oval, and set obliquely. Dark in colour, except in the case of Chocolates, which may be lighter, and in Dapples, one or both wall eyes are permissible.

EARS, value 5 : Broad, of moderate length and well rounded (not narrow, pointed, or folded), relatively well back, high and well set on, lying close to the cheek, very mobile as in all intelligent dogs, when at attention the back of the ear directed forward and outward.

JAW, value 5 : Neither too square nor snipey, but strong, lips lightly stretched, fairly covering the lower jaw.

NECK, value 3 : Sufficiently long, muscular, clean, no dewlap, slightly arched in the nape, running in graceful lines into the shoulders, carried well up and forward.

FOREQUARTERS, value 10 : Shoulder blades long, broad, and set on sloping, lying firmly on fully developed ribs or thorax, muscles hard and plastic. Chest very oval, with ample room for heart and lungs, deep and well sprung out ribs towards the loins, breast bone prominent.

LEGS AND FEET, value 25 : Forelegs very short and in proportion to size, strong in bone. Upper arm of equal length with, and at right angles to shoulder blade, elbows lying close to ribs but moving freely up to shoulder blades. Lower arm short as compared with other animals, slightly inclined inwards (crook), seen in profile moderately straight, not bending forward or knuckling over (unsoundness), feet large, round and strong with thick pads, toes compact and with distinct arch in each toe, nails strong. The dogs must stand true, *i.e.*, equally on all parts of the foot.

BODY TRUNK, value 9 : Long and muscular, the line of back slightly depressed at shoulders and slightly arched over loin, which should be short and strong, outline of belly moderately tucked up.

HINDQUARTERS, value 10 : Rump round, full, broad ; muscles hard and plastic, hip-bone or pelvis bone not too short, broad and strongly developed, set moderately sloping ; thigh bones strong, of good length and joined to pelvis at right angles ; lower thighs short in comparison with other animals ; hocks well developed and seen from behind the legs should be straight (not cowhocked), hind feet smaller in bone and narrower than fore feet. The dog should not appear higher at quarters than at shoulders.

STERN, value 5 ; Set on fairly high, strong and tapering, but not too long and not too much curved nor carried too high.

COAT AND SKIN, value 3 : Short, dense and smooth, but strong. The hair on the underside of the tail coarse in texture, skin loose and supple.

COLOUR, value 3 : Any colour. No white except spot on breast. Nose and sinal should be black. In red dogs a red nose is permissable, but not desirable. In Chocolates and Dapples the nose may be brown or flesh coloured. In Dapples large spots of colour are undesirable, and the dog should be evenly dappled all over.

WEIGHT : Heavy-weight dogs not exceeding 25 lbs. Heavy-weight bitches not exceeding 23 lbs. Light-weight Dogs not exceeding 21 lbs. Light-weight bitches not exceeding 19 lbs.

FAULTS : In general appearance weak or deformed, too high or too low to the ground : Ears set on too high or too low ; Eyes too prominent ; Muzzle too short or pinched, neither undershot nor overshot ; Forelegs too much crooked or with hare or terrier feet, or flat spread toes (flat-footed), out at elbows ; Body too much dip behind the shoulders ; Loins weak or too much arched ; Chest too flat or too short ; Hindquarters weak or cowhocked and hips higher than shoulders. It is recommended that in judging Dachshunds the above-mentioned negative points (faults) should only be penalized to the extent of the values allotted to such positive points.

A LAMENT FOR THE DACHSHUND

The Drawer of Badgers—The Sussex Squire and his Bell-mouthed Beagles—A Real 'Rabbity Day'—And a New Use for the Dachshund.

THERE IS A LAMENT for the dachshund. His lovers complain that he is a miserable drawing-room pet. This is true. I have never seen a dachshund bite a rabbit. But he was bred and brought up to bite badgers. Hence his name. *Dachs* is German for 'badger,' and *Hund* is, naturally, the basis of our English word 'hound.'

The dachshund was bred with short legs, a long body, incisor teeth, and trap-like, pointed jaws in order that he might follow the badger into the farthest, darkest subterranean caverns of his 'sett,' and thence drive him forth into the broad daylight and the iron tongs of the badger-digger—a job which is performed in England by miserable but lion-hearted terriers.

Thus we witness the declining glory of the sleek 'sausage dog.' Born a fighter, bred a warrior, nurtured on Nordic aims of war, he has become a mere paddler about carpets, a licker-up of chocolates, a sycophant at women's knees. So the days of dogs decline. The fighter has fallen. The drawer of badgers has become a lowly squire of dames.

But I am perhaps a little hard on the dachshund. For all his drawing-room popularity he is a gallant little dog, happy in a sunny ditch-bottom on a mild autumn afternoon when the ferrets are working, the rats bolting. Run the fat off him, and he will twist and snap, turn and chase, almost with the best of the terriers. Put him, singly or by the half-dozen, into a square of gorse on a slope of downland that falls verdant into the sparkling Sussex sea, stand at one corner, gun-barrels balanced lightly, ready for the instant shot, and hear the badger-dog drawing through the gorse, weaving in and out like a serpent, sudden terror to the rabbits which dwell therein. They soon bolt, and you will get those grand, flat-out shots when Brer Rabbit, hit clean in the head, does a double somersault down the slope, to finish up twitching, white belly uppermost.

Years ago there was a Sussex squire who regularly used a pack of the old slow-footed, bell-mouthed Sussex beagles for such rabbit days. He put bells on their collars. The bracken on his downland slopes was rided into broad squares.

The old squire would collect his friends, his ruddy-faced neighbours in beaver hats and buskins, his tenant farmers in brass-buttoned, green cutaways and kersey-mere breeches. They turned up from miles, in dog-carts and gigs, tooling along the white, dusty Sussex lanes, their long-barrelled guns between their knees, for the great rabbit day of the year.

For twenty-four hours beforehand the head keeper, his men and boys, had stunk out every rabbit-hole within a square mile. The party gathered at the chalky gateway which opened between grass-grown, bracken-covered banks on to the down that fell in verdant folds to the cliff's edge, where sparkled the sea to the rim of the sky. There was a great sorting out of cartridges, flasks, even shot-belts, for one or two still used the long-barrelled muzzle-loader; a flying back and forth of greetings between neighbours, chucklings over past days, rumbling jokes at easy shots missed last twelvemonth but still remembered.

Then the beagles turned up, a motley, particoloured, magpie-looking lot, undulating down the narrow lane, their little bells tinkling. Somehow they provoked a sudden, fantastic image of undersized sheep.

Rabbits lay out on the turf by the hundred, some crouching, some sitting bolt upright, ears cocked, eyes alert for the commotion at the gateway, the march of men and dogs that presaged war.

Then the party moved off. The rabbits scuttled to cover. Guns drew lots, took up their positions. The beagles were put in. The chime of little bells broke musically on the sunny morning. Then the first rabbits were afoot. The bell-mouthed chorus crashed out.

Presently they began to bolt. Shot after shot rang out. The heavy bang of black powder echoed across the empty downs. A blue haze of pre-smokeless powder hung thinly on the air, stung the nostrils sharply. Soon it was a crackling, irregular volley. The turf was alive with racing rabbits, fireworky with rabbits which turned sudden somersaults, catapulted themselves a foot into the air in the death-spring. It was dotted with rabbits that lay dead.

So the morning went on. It was the day of the

sheep-farmer's revenge, the ultimate answer to acres of green turf nibbled down to the chalk. And at midday they gathered in a sunny quarry, their backs to sun-warmed chalk, sand-martens dodging in and out of their holes, a kestrel swinging high in the blue. Cold rabbit and bacon pie, great wicker-covered jars of home brew, home-made cake, Ribston pippins that crackled sweetly on the teeth, cheese whose memory lingers like a dream, pats of yellow butter, and great flat, crusty loaves, still smelling of the wood ashes. That was the high point of the day, crowned if you wished with a glass or two of the squire's ' put-wine.'

Nobody shoots rabbits on sunny Sussex downlands with such packs of slow and musical beagles in these hurried days. We hurry so much we miss the half of life, the charm of the quiet things, the simplicity of the easily attainable.

Perhaps one could not even find the like of such slow-footed, bell-mouthed beagles, with their heavy ears, their loving, sleepy eyes, to-day. I dare say they have been show-benched into a Never-Never Land, a land peopled by the misty dreams of old-fashioned sportsmen who have no use and less wonderment for dog-show poodledom.

But it was a pleasant way of shooting rabbits. It combined a smack of hunting with the quickness and zest of real snap-shooting. So if we cannot find the beagles, why not turn the dachshund to this very simple form of sport? I will bet a last year's hat that he would like it. It would revive in his lowly breast the dormant Teutonic ardour of the chase. Who knows but that the grey shape of the crouching rabbit might not wake some atavistic dream of far-off generations of German brocks! Surely it is fair to the dachshund to give him this humble chance of recovering his lost manhood.

I have a suspicion, more than a suspicion, that the dachshund derives from the French basset hound. Of course, there are dachs fans who will tell you that if you gaze into the tombs of two-thousand-year-old Egyptian ladies you will see sculptured the profiles of the faithful dachshund. But I have gazed into these tombs, and I cannot believe that the prick-eared, coffin-headed, jackal-like little beasts there delineated have anything to do with the dachshund we love to-day.

I prefer to stick to the basset-hound theory. That dead-and-gone writer "Wildfowler," who discoursed so learnedly on duck-shooting and dogs, delivered in the first edition of *British Dogs* the following opinion:

" . . . A black-and-tan or red basset *à jambes torses* cannot, by any possible use of one's eyes, be distinguished from a dachshund of the same colour, although some German writers assert that the breeds are quite distinct. To the naked eye there is no difference; but in the matter of names (wherein German scientists particularly shine), then, indeed, confusion gets worse confounded. They have, say, a dozen black-and-tan bassets *à jambes torses* before them. Well, if one of them is a thoroughly good-looking hound they call him *Dachs Bracken*; if he is short-eared and with a pointed muzzle they cap him with the appellation of *Dachshund*. Between you and me, kind reader, it is a distinction without a difference, and there is no doubt they both belong to the same breed. I will, at a fortnight's notice, place a basset *à jambes torses*, small size, side by side with the best dachshund hound to be found, and if any difference in legs, anatomy, and general appearance of the two can be detected I shall be very greatly surprised."

But then, in a later chapter on the dachshund, he produces the following bombshell:

"The head, when of proper [dachshund] type, greatly resembles that of a bloodhound. The ears are also long and pendulous; . . . the muzzle should finish square, and the flews should be fairly developed. . . . We have a brood bitch from one of the best kennels in Germany in which the dewlap is very strongly pronounced. . . . The forelegs are one of the great peculiarities of the breed: these are very large in bone for the size of the dog, and very crooked, being turned out at the elbows and in at the knees. . . . The feet should be very large, and should be well splayed outwards."

I wonder where one would find a bloodhound-headed dachshund to-day!

The breed is probably about two hundred years old, and in England it dates from about 1850. Somewhere in the sixties it poked its long nose into the boudoirs of Queen Victoria and the Princess of Wales, later Queen Alexandra. Its popularity was immediate, and from Royal circles the snaky 'sausage dog' permeated downward through the aristocracy to the ranks of the common or show-bench exhibitors. I believe the first event which actually gave separate classes for the breed was the show at the Crystal Palace in 1873. From that day to the present the dachshund has grown steadily in popularity. The first champion that I can discover was Mrs Merrick Hoare's Dessauer, bred by Count Picked, a black-and-tan dog which she imported into this country in 1874. Then there was Mr Arkwright's famous old Champion Xaverl, who came to England in 1876, direct from the Royal kennels at Stuttgart. These two, with Champion Jackdaw, a descendant of Xaverl, are really the cornerstones of the breed in England to-day.

The wretched dachshund suffered severely during the War. It is odd, after a lapse of years, to reflect that because of his Germanic ancestry the harmless, friendly dachs was subjected to an actual and literal hymn of hate between the years 1914 and 1919. One well-known judge of the breed was furiously attacked by a gang of toughs in a Scottish town in 1915, because he had walked down the street leading a dachshund bitch. The dog was only saved from lynching by the arrival of the police.

I am far from being a wholehearted believer in show-bench or field-trial standards of points as the ultimate criterion of the working qualities of any dog. Too much has been made of the importance of these machine-made standards within the last twenty or thirty years. In some cases rigid adherence to show-bench rules and points may even lead to a definite deterioration in a breed. But every sensible person recognizes that a standard of points is necessary, if only as a definite framework on which the future development of the breed must be founded.

So here is the modern standard of points, adopted by the English Dachshund Club, after the old standard had been cancelled in 1907. This new standard follows the basis laid down by the Teckel Klub of Germany in 1891, and applies to smooth-haired dachshunds only. The wire-haired, long-haired, and miniature dachshunds are sufficiently rare for me to deny them space which they might legitimately claim in a more specialized work. Here is the up-to-date standard of points for the smooth dachshund:

General Appearance. Long and low, but with compact and well-muscled body, neither crippled, cloddy, nor clumsy, with bold, defiant carriage of head and intelligent expression.   10 *points*

Head and Skull. Long and appearing conical when seen from above and from a side view, tapering to the point of the muzzle. Stop not pronounced, and skull slightly arched in profile and appearing neither too broad nor too narrow.   9 *points*

Eyes. Medium in size, oval, and set obliquely. Dark in colour, except in the case of chocolates, in which they may be lighter, and in dapples, in which one or both wall eyes are permissible.   3 *points*

Ears. Broad, of moderate length, and well rounded (not narrow, pointed, or folded), relatively well back, high, and well set on, lying close to the cheek, very mobile; when at attention the back of the ear directed forward and outward.   5 *points*

Jaw. Neither too square nor snipy, but strong; lips lightly stretched and fairly covering lower jaw. 5 *points*

Neck. Sufficiently long, muscular, clean, showing no dewlap, slightly arched in the nape, running in graceful lines into the shoulder, carried well up and forward. 3 *points*

Forequarters. Shoulder-blades long, broad, and set on sloping, lying firmly on fully developed ribs or thorax, muscles hard and plastic. Chest very oval, with ample room for heart and lungs, deep, and with the ribs well sprung out towards the loin, breast-bone prominent. 10 *points*

Legs and Feet. Forelegs very short and, in proportion to size, strong in bone. Upper arm of equal length with, and at right angles to, the shoulder-blade; elbows lying close to the ribs, but moving freely up to shoulder-blades. Lower arm short as compared with other animals, slightly inclined inwards (crook), seen in profile moderately straight, not bending forward nor knuckling over; feet large, round, and strong, with thick pads; toes compact and with distinct arch in each toe; nails strong. The dog must stand true—*i.e.,* equally on all parts of the foot. 25 *points*

Body or Trunk. Long and muscular, the line of the back slightly depressed at shoulders and slightly arched over loin, which should be short and strong; outline of belly moderately tucked up. 9 *points*

Hindquarters. Rump round, full, broad; muscles hard and plastic; hip-bone, or pelvis, not too short, broad, and strongly developed, set moderately sloping; thigh bones strong, of good length, and joined to the pelvis at right angles. Lower thighs short in comparison with other animals; hocks well developed and, seen from behind the legs, should be straight (not cow-hocked). Hind-feet smaller in bone and narrower than forefeet. The dog should not appear higher at the quarters than at the shoulders. 10 *points*

(1) THE DACHSHUND IS STILL IN ROYAL FAVOUR

Here is the King's Warrener ferreting in Windsor Park with one in attendance.

(2) A GOOD SPECIMEN OF THE ATTRACTIVE LONG-HAIRED
DACHSHUND

Mr R. E. Chamberlain's 'Nathaniel of Stutton.'

Photos Sport and General

"SLIPPED!"

Mrs Oliver Lucas's 'Blondie Locks' and Lieut.-Colonel Heseltine's 'Joe's Hunger' being slipped in the Sussex Oaks at the South of England Coursing Club's meeting at Woodhorne Farm, Bognor Regis, in 1937.

Photo Sport and General

Stern. Set on fairly high, strong and tapering, but not too long and not too much curved or carried too high. *5 points*

Coat and Skin. Short, dense, and smooth, but strong. The hair on the under-side of the tail coarse in texture. Skin loose and supple. *3 points*

Colour. Any colour. No white except spot on breast. Nose and sinal should be black. In red dogs a red nose is permissible, but not desirable. In chocolates and dapples the nose may be brown or flesh-coloured. In dapples large spots of colour are undesirable; the dog should be evenly dappled all over. *3 points*

Weight. Heavy-weights: up to 25 lb. for dogs, and up to 23 lb. for bitches. Light-weights: up to 21 lb. for dogs, and up to 19 lb. for bitches.

There, then, are the points which should give any ordinary supporter of the breed as much common-sense guidance as he desires so far as the smooth-haired type is concerned.

One final word of advice is worth remembering: that is, that if you want a dachshund to be of any use as a sporting dog it is no good having one with a mincing, dancing gait. This may look all very well in the house, but it is not the slightest use in the field. A dachshund which is to be a sporting dog must have a free, easy, swinging gait, throw its legs forward with a smooth, flowing motion, plenty of room between the hocks, nothing wobbly or unsteady. So if you are going to buy a dachshund for fun as well as decoration, have him trotted out and walked round just as you would with a horse. It is worth the extra five minutes of observation.

Lightning Source UK Ltd.
Milton Keynes UK
30 December 2010

165004UK00001B/54/P